woven to wear

17 THOUGHTFUL DESIGNS
WITH SIMPLE SHAPES

MARILYN MURPHY

INTERWEAVE.
interweave.com

EDITOR: Madelyn van der Hoogt
TECHNICAL EDITOR: Diane Kelly
ART DIRECTOR: Liz Quan
WARDROBE STYLIST: Emily Choi
HAIR AND MAKEUP: Kathy MacKay
DESIGNER: Julia Boyles
PRODUCTION: Katherine Jackson
ILLUSTRATOR: Missy Shepler
PHOTOGRAPHY: Joe Hancock (model images, except where noted) and Robert L. Medlock (process images)

Interweave Press LLC
A division of F+W Media, Inc.
201 East Fourth Street
Loveland, CO 80537
interweave.com

Manufactured in China by Asia Pacific Offset Ltd.

Library of Congress Cataloging-in-Publication Data

Murphy, Marilyn.
 Woven to wear : 17 thoughtful designs with simple shapes / Marilyn Murphy.
   pages cm
  ISBN 978-1-59668-651-9 (pbk.)
  ISBN 978-1-59668-927-5 (PDF)
 1. Hand weaving. 2. Clothing and dress. I. Title.
  TT848.M865 2013
  746.1'4041--dc23

                                    2012048056

10 9 8 7 6 5 4 3 2 1

ACKNOWLEDGMENTS

TO MY MOTHER. Little did she know when she placed a wind-up music box that played "Baa baa black sheep" into my hands at a young age and later bought me a pot-holder loom that she set the course of my life's journey. A thank-you is hardly enough.

TO LINDA LIGON and the press she created. Without Interweave, I wouldn't be sitting here writing this, and many weavers would never have learned to weave. I have deep gratitude for Linda's "just do it" mindset and all her encouragement and support, but most of all for years of friendship.

TO AVIS MOELLER, my college professor of clothing and textiles, who taught me about fabric and design and our continued shared passion for ethnic dress and its influences.

TO MADELYN VAN DER HOOGT, master weaver, teacher, and editor of my words. Her good nature, humor, and support got me through it; her crafting and careful editing of all made it a better book for you to learn from and enjoy.

TO MY INTERN CARRIE RORVIG, who wound warps, threaded looms, wove, stitched, modeled, and provided invaluable feedback on what she as a student weaver would want to know.

TO THE TALENTED INTERWEAVE STAFF whom I've had the privilege of working with for many years—you taught me so much.

TO MY CLOTHROADS PARTNERS, Suzanne DeAtley, Dee Lockwood, and Linda Tiley Stark, who tolerated me through a year of taking my eye off the business. May we always share deep roots with our global textile artisans.

TO THE YARN COMPANIES who provided yarn for this book and continue to provide top service to so many makers, to the local yarn stores for continuing on in spite of the Internet age, and to all my yarn-store customers who took up the shuttle to learn this noble craft.

And last, with the deepest gratitude, **TO MY HUSBAND ROBERT MEDLOCK,** who supported me in countless ways through this entire endeavor and many others.

A thoughtful and heart-full thank-you to all.

CONTENTS

Introduction

Much contemporary clothing design shows the influence of ethnic and tribal wear in a global melting pot of traditional folkloric costume and ethnic fabrics. Silhouettes are roomy, layered, and flowing. These elements translate beautifully into simple garment styles using handwoven fabrics with a rich use of color and pattern and out-of-the-ordinary detailing. This collection of woven wearables is inspired by traditional cloth and clothing from around the world.

Although *Woven to Wear* gives complete directions for weaving and sewing the garments featured here, this book is much more than a project book. Included with the projects are many how-to tips for producing the fabric you want through yarn and color selection, techniques for designing styles and shapes and creating your own garment patterns, and step-by-step instructions for assembly, sewing, and finishing techniques—all useful skills that you can apply to any handwoven apparel.

Even more, to inspire all of us I invited nine other handwoven clothing designers to contribute to *Woven to Wear*. All of them have specialized in garment design for most of their weaving careers. Each offers a unique perspective. You'll learn what inspires them and how they approach the fabric and garment-making process as well as become inspired by their designs—all of which you can use for your own journey.

Nancy Waight Paap is a self-taught weaver whose designs are influenced by the beauty of the Southwest. She weaves intuitively, letting yarn, color, and texture take center stage. Layna Bentley utilizes a design-as-you-go process. She weaves narrow pieces for a single garment, changing from piece to piece as ideas come. She has a penchant for using scrap fabrics from one garment as parts of the next. In contrast to these two designers, Joyce Wilkerson is very deliberate in her approach, keeping files of sources of inspiration, planning colorful warps with computer software, and developing a yearly line of varied garments that are all woven on the same warp.

> Handwoven garments with simple lines are perfect palettes for fine detailing and finishing touches.

If you're a surface designer and understand the principles of chemical reactions that occur with dye and fiber, then there's even more creative play open to you in garment design. Teri D. Inman was influenced by the Japanese pole wrap-and-dye technique of arashi shibori and now uses that as the basis of her work. Elizabeth Jenkins creates uniquely patterned cloth with a discharging process. And Liz Spear works collaboratively with other fiber artists who marble on her cloth or create special hand-dyed yarns for her to use. Currently, she is incorporating nuno felting into her work.

Handwoven garments with simple lines are perfect palettes for fine detailing and finishing touches. Jean S. Jones focuses on very fine sewing using many handsewing techniques. Heather Winslow adds intricate braided, crocheted, and knitted edges. Anita Luvera Mayer uses surface treatments (embroidery, beading, rya, crochet, and more) to embellish her woven garments.

Any woven project starts with a desire to make something that can be worn—whether to show it off, to give us warmth, or simply to wrap around us. The process that follows the desire takes time and thought. The very fact that we can create a unique fabric for a specific purpose in a world that values instant gratification is truly special. But where and how do *you* begin?

Design ideas are everywhere. You don't need formal training to pay attention to what surrounds you. You need some slow time to take in what you see, to record it, and—with some practice—to interpret what you see into cloth and shapes. You need a passion for making things by hand.

It was this passion that drove me to take my first real-job earnings after college and buy a floor loom. I would race home from work during my lunch hour to weave scarves and shawls. From this beginning, a friend and I developed a line of high-end handwoven clothing and accessories at a time when the word "handwoven" brought images of 1960s shapes and fabrics to the minds of buyers.

Then I bought the Weaving Workshop in Chicago. It was there I really learned about yarn and its making and what could be created with it. I taught (and learned) the ins and outs of weaving cloth by hand. A later move to Colorado extended my weaving knowledge into the editing and publishing world of magazines and books at Interweave. Even as this world absorbed my time, I continued to think about handwoven cloth and fashion. I stored it all in files labeled "artists," "inspiration," and "wearables." I saved my portfolios, sketchbooks, and teaching notes. I collected ethnic fabrics and scarves. I tagged blogs and images online. And finally I slowed down enough to use these notes and weave!

So that's my weaving story. I hope there are nuggets you relate to. But most of all, I hope that the designs and information shared in these pages will assist you in developing your own signature style and ignite (or reignite) your passion for creating handwoven wearables.

CHAPTER 1

Getting Started

Weaving a garment requires more skills, space, and tools than crocheting, knitting, or even sewing does. As with them, however, both sides of the brain must work together: the right side for creative visioning and holistic thinking and the left side for figuring out all the steps needed to make the vision a reality.

Weavers of wearables must acquire both weaving and basic sewing skills as well as materials and equipment and the space to put them in. Although the projects in this book were woven on a floor loom (which takes up space even if it can be folded up), most can be woven on a simple rigid-heddle loom that can be easily stored. Weavers have been creating elegant clothing on narrow, simple looms for centuries and still do so today in cultures that maintain a weaving tradition. Edgings, shaping, yarn choices, color effects, embellishments, and other treatments can turn simple cloth into uniquely beautiful garments.

Skills
CROCHET AND KNITTING

Many weavers are multicrafters who also know other fiber-related hand skills. For garment making, crochet is handy for finishing edges, seaming garments, making collars and cuffs, and adding trims; knitting can be used for trims and ribbings. For the garments in this book, if you don't know how to crochet or knit, you can collaborate with a friend who does or you can finish garment edges in other ways.

Single crochet.

Knitted ribbing.

Sewing a zigzag edge.

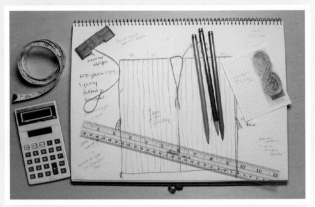

Planning tools.

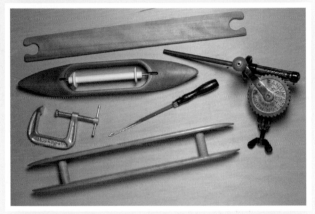

Weaving equipment.

SEWING

You'll need only very basic sewing skills for these garments: joining seams and sewing hems using a tapestry needle and yarn, attaching snaps and buttons with a needle and sewing thread, and machine straight stitching or zigzagging fabric edges to prevent raveling. If you don't have a sewing machine, you can substitute handsewing where machine stitching is recommended, as shown in Finishing, pages 120–122.

WEAVING

All but one of the projects in this book are woven in plain weave and therefore require only two shafts; most of these can be woven on a rigid-heddle loom. You'll need only basic weaving skills: winding a warp, threading the loom, reading a draft, following warp and weft color orders, and weaving with a consistent beat and smooth selvedges.

Equipment
PLANNING TOOLS

You'll need a few tools to use for planning. A calculator, a handy app on your smartphone, and/or spreadsheet software on a computer are all useful for calculating warp and weft amounts and other weaving-related numbers. You'll need a ruler for drawing straight lines and doing yarn wraps to determine sett (or you can use an inch gauge for this), graph paper for planning layouts, and a sketchbook for jotting down ideas and designs.

WEAVING EQUIPMENT

In addition to a loom, you'll need a warping board or warping pegs (for short warps), a threading hook, the reed or rigid heddle specified in the project, lease sticks and/or raddle (depending on your warping method), and corrugated cardboard or smooth warping sticks to separate layers of warp and cloth on the beams. Boat shuttles make weaving faster (thus requiring bobbins and a bobbin winder), though you can use stick shuttles instead. For bulky, textured wefts, I like to use rug shuttles. A few miscellaneous items specific to particular projects are two C-clamps and a few yards of monofilament (fishing line).

SEWING EQUIPMENT

Some of these items are not strictly sewing equipment, but they're used for designing and fitting the garments.

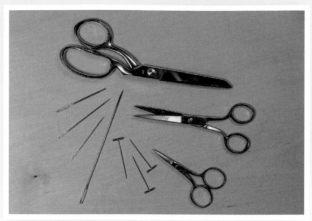

Sewing equipment.

- ✤ **A full-length mirror** to see how a garment looks proportionally on your body.

- ✤ **A dress form** for fitting (or if you have a friend who is close to your size and height, you can do fitting of sample garments on her).

- ✤ **A sewing machine** for straight and zigzag stitching to secure raw edges (or you can use a serger or finish fabric edges by hand).

- ✤ **Needles** Sewing needles with sharp points as well as blunt-end tapestry needles in various sizes for different weights of cloth; straight and T-pins.

- ✤ **Sharp embroidery scissors** for cutting yarns and threads, dressmaker's shears for cutting cloth, medium-size scissors for other tasks, and paper scissors for cutting out patterns.

- ✤ **Miscellaneous** Sewing thread to match the yarn, a tape measure for measuring body parts and cloth during weaving and afterward, card stock (or old file folders) for making neck templates, butcher paper or brown paper for making flat patterns, a masking-tape roller for quickly picking up bits of yarns off the table, and (very optional but I love these) fabric weights to hold down the pattern on the cloth (you can use these in place of pinning) and to hold down a woven piece when tying fringe or working an edge treatment.

Finishing equipment.

FINISHING EQUIPMENT

(See Finishing, pages 118–125, for how to use this equipment.)

- ✤ **Washing** I use a front-loading washing machine because it doesn't agitate the fabric as much as a top loader does. You can also wash all fabrics by hand in a large basin or bathtub.

- ✤ **Pressing** An ironing board and fabric steamer or steam iron.

- ✤ **Miscellaneous** Assorted crochet hooks and circular knitting needles, a nylon-bristle brush for raising the nap on cloth, and a stash of unusual buttons.

MATERIALS

Collect various weights and types of woven fabrics for making muslins (sample garments for testing shape, fit, sleeve and neck-opening placement, lengths, and other elements), in the same weight as the handwoven fabric used for the garment; note that knitted or interlocked fabrics won't drape the same way handwoven ones do. Look for old bed sheets or blankets from second-hand and thrift stores and sale fabrics from fabric stores.

For specifics about yarn, see Yarn, pages 11–15.

To work with yarn for weaving if it comes in skeins, you'll need a skein winder and a ball winder (or use a chair flipped on its side, so its legs can become a handy "holder," and wind the yarn into a pull ball by hand).

WORKSPACE

Not everyone is fortunate enough to have a dedicated weaving/sewing studio. An efficient workspace is one where you have both your weaving and sewing area all in one room, or at least close by each other. It has taken me years to have such a place so that I no longer have to take the sewing machine off the kitchen table to eat, and my loom isn't in the dining room in place of a table. It doesn't mean I'm a better weaver. It does mean I can leave work in progress, close the door, and be ready to start working again when time permits.

If space and resources are limited, make sure you have a large flat work surface for your sewing machine, for laying out cloth and cutting fabric, and just for general planning. This can be a rectangular dining or kitchen table or a folding worktable that can be stored when not in use.

Good lighting is a must. Natural lighting isn't always possible, so replace your bulbs with daylight ones to see colors accurately as well as avoid eyestrain. A portable clamp light that can be moved around is very handy when extra lighting is needed for close-up work.

Reading Drafts

In a draft for weaving, the horizontal rows across the top represent the shafts. Each number in a row represents one warp end threaded through a heddle on that shaft. The columns at the right of the threading (the tie-up) represent the treadles and show which shafts are "tied" to go up when each treadle is used. The marks in the columns below the treadling show which treadle to use for each weft pick.

All but one of the projects in this book are woven in plain weave. If you have a 2-shaft loom, thread shafts 1 and 2 alternately following the 2-shaft draft shown below. If you have a 4-shaft loom, thread the shafts in straight order following the 4-shaft draft and then weave by raising shafts 1 and 3 (treadle 1) alternating with shafts 2 and 4 (treadle 2).

The Crème de la Crème Poncho is the only project in this book that is not plain weave. The draft for it is a bit more complicated; part of it is shown in the right-hand draft below. The letters in the threading and treadling indicate which yarns to use. Thread shafts 1-2-3-4 and repeat that threading using the wool (W) yarn. In the treadling, brackets serve as a shorthand to tell you how many times to repeat a particular treadling order. With roving (R), for example, alternate treadles 3 and 4 three times. Now alternate treadles 3 and 4 with the novelty (N) yarn two times, with roving (R) two times, weave 3 picks of bouclé (B) as shown, and alternate treadles 3 and 4 with roving (R) two times. Repeat the entire section enclosed within the "4x" brackets four times.

Drafts for Weaving

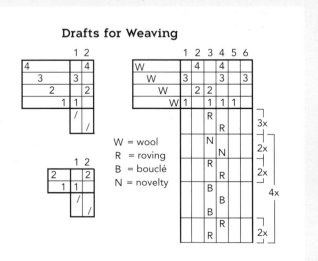

W = wool
R = roving
B = bouclé
N = novelty

Reading a Warp and Weft Color Order

A Warp Color Order looks like a threading draft but instead indicates the order in which to wind warp colors. You can read the chart from either side; usually we read from right to left. To follow the Warp Color Order shown here, wind 4 black, 8 green, 4 black, then 9 red alternating with 9 white repeated six times, and end with 4 green, 4 black. A Weft Color Order is read from top to bottom the way a treadling draft is read; brackets indicate the number of times to repeat a section. For the Weft Color Order shown here, weave 66 picks cranberry, then *33 yellow, 36 cranberry, 33 green, 36 cranberry, 33 orange, 36 cranberry; repeat from * six times and end with 33 yellow, 66 cranberry.

Using a Rigid-Heddle Loom

Most of the projects in this book can be woven using a rigid-heddle loom. You'll need a rigid heddle that can produce the number of ends per inch and the weaving width required by the project. If the project requires a 6-dent reed for 6 ends per inch, for example, you'll need what is often called a 6-dent rigid heddle (three slot/hole pairs equal 1" of warp width). In this book, the Blooming Scarf, the Checkered Sweater, and the Loopy Tabard take a 6-dent rigid heddle; the Quechquemitl Wrap, the Shades of Green Vest, and the Ribbon Scarf take an 8-dent rigid heddle; the Sherbet Shrug, the Striped Mohair Shawl, and the Plaid Cowl take a 10-dent rigid heddle; and the Wabi Sabi Jacket takes a 12-dent rigid heddle. (A rigid-heddle loom not only has the advantage of being portable, but it also produces less loom waste than a floor loom.)

Some Terms to Know

❖ **Draw-in** The percentage of width lost (from the width in the reed) to accommodate the weft's interlacement with the warp during weaving and when tension is released (for the projects in this book, this percentage is given under Take-Up and Shrinkage).

Warp Color Order

	6x			
12	4		4	4 black
12	4			8 green
54		9		red
54	9			white
132				

Weft Color Order

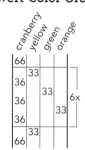

❖ **Loom waste** The part of the warp that is wasted, usually referring to the amount used to tie onto the front apron rod plus the amount left on the loom when the fabric is cut off.

❖ **Sett** The number of warp threads (warp sett) and/or weft threads (weft sett) per inch. The warp sett is usually described as the number of ends per inch (epi); the weft sett as the number of picks per inch (ppi).

❖ **Shrinkage** The percentage by which the fabric becomes smaller from wet-finishing. (Note that in the layouts, numbers in parentheses indicate fabric measurements after wet-finishing.)

❖ **Take-up** The percentage of actual warp length lost to accommodate interlacement with the weft when tension is released. This amount varies, based on setts, weave structure, and yarn.

❖ **Waste yarn** A yarn used as the weft to weave a header or to weave areas that will become fringe or areas that separate pieces from each other. Waste yarn is removed, either when the cloth is removed from the loom or after wet-finishing (see page 15).

CHAPTER 2

Yarn

Do you buy yarn for a specific project or do you see a special yarn, buy it, and then plan the project? Probably you do both—and the yarn gets added to your "stash." As a yarn lover, you may also find irresistible the explosion of colorful novelty yarns currently produced for knitters, so skeins of these yarns find their way to your shelves, too. Sooner or later, you'll want to try combining some of them with weaving yarns in the same fabric, mixing one skein of this and another of that. To do this for a "wow" cloth with just the right hand, it's helpful to understand general fiber and yarn properties.

Some Terms to Know

❖ **Abrasion** Wearing or rubbing away because of friction. Yarns for weaving must be able to resist abrasion or they will fuzz up, weaken, or even break during warping and weaving and may also pill in the final fabric.

❖ **Absorbency** The ability of a fiber to soak up moisture. This is especially important for drawing perspiration from your body but feeling dry on your skin.

❖ **Drape** Drape is affected by spin, ply, and degree of twist as well as fiber content, sett, and weave structure. The drape of a fabric relates to how a cloth hangs on the body.

❖ **Elasticity** The degree to which a yarn returns to its original length after elongation. Some yarns are elastic, some are inelastic, and still others are damaged by tension, never returning to their original state.

❖ **Strength** The ability of a yarn to withstand tension. Will it weaken or break during weaving or wet-finishing?

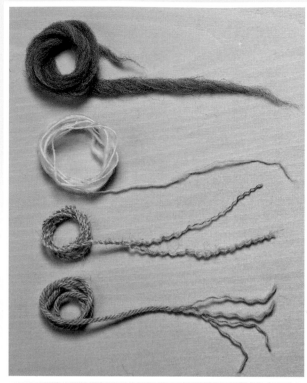

Wool yarn (top to bottom): roving, thick-and-thin singles, 2-ply, 4-ply.

Types of Yarns

Fiber content and yarn construction affect all aspects of planning, warping, weaving, and wet-finishing.

❖ **Singles vs plied** A singles yarn is a fiber spun into one strand. A few projects in this book use a singles yarn or even roving (unspun fiber). Unless a singles yarn is spun tightly (such as the tweed yarn in the Checkered Sweater), it should not be used for warp. It has little strength and can easily be abraded. Plied yarns are two or more spun strands twisted together and are stronger than a singles. Plied yarns can also be plied with each other to make a thicker and/or stronger yarn.

❖ **Slippery yarns** Some yarns, such as bamboo, rayon and rayon blends, Tencel, and silk, have a slippery surface. They are therefore slippery throughout the warping and weaving processes. Use more choke ties to secure the warp. If you are threading front to back, tie off sections of the threaded warp so the ends don't slip out of the reed before you thread the heddles.

Fiber content and yarn construction affect all aspects of planning, warping, weaving, and wet-finishing.

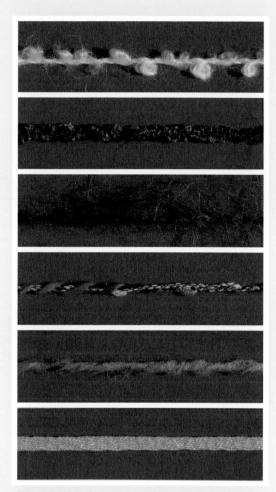

Top to bottom: bouclé, chenille, brushed mohair, nub, tweed, ribbon.

❖ **Loop** A variation of bouclé in which the loops are regular in size and spacing.

Can bouclé or loop yarns be used as warp? "It depends" is the only answer. The core must have a tight enough twist or be plied so that the bouclé doesn't come undone while it is under tension on the loom. Test by applying tension to both ends of a strand about a yard long to see if you can pull the yarn apart. Sampling is also important. I usually use bouclé and loop yarns in combination with other nontextured yarns in the warp to add support.

❖ **Chenille** A yarn made by first weaving a cloth using pairs of very fine warp threads with spaces between the pairs and thick, soft, closely sett weft threads. The "cloth" is then cut along the spaces into warpwise strips, which become the chenille yarn.

Chenille yarns produce a fabric that feels like velvet after washing. Setts need to be fairly close, as the structure of the yarn allows for more compactness.

❖ **Brushed mohair** Mohair is a yarn spun from the hair of an Angora goat. It is available as a smooth plied yarn or as a brushed yarn. Brushing is a process that frees tiny hairs along the yarn's length.

These hairs stick to each other, so when you are using brushed mohair for warp, sley it at fewer ends per inch than for other yarns of similar yards per pound (see the Striped Mohair Shawl, Plaid Cowl, and Sherbet Shrug). Sampling is always key before you decide to use mohair as a primary warp yarn.

❖ **Nub** A 2-ply or 3-ply yarn in which tufts of fiber are caught between the turns of the ply. Nubby yarns can get caught in the reed if the dents are too narrow. To test a yarn, glide it back and forth through a dent. If it sticks, change to a reed with fewer dents per inch and sley more ends per dent. Some nubby yarns can't handle the usual abrasion from the reed and heddles that weaving requires.

❖ **Tweed** Usually refers to a singles yarn with small tufts of fiber inserted randomly and held in place by the twist of the yarn. A tweed yarn can also be a plied yarn, in which case the tufts of fiber are held more firmly in place by the plies.

❖ **Woolen vs worsted** The difference between woolen and worsted yarns is a difference in spinning method and length of staple. Woolen yarns are spun from carded rolags of a short staple, so the short fibers wrap around each other to make a lofty yarn. Most yarns used by weavers are woolen spun because the natural crimp of the fiber remains, allowing it to full when wet-finished. Worsted yarns are spun from combed wool fibers with long staples that run parallel to each other, leaving little or no natural crimp. Worsted yarns are strong and appropriate for outer garments, rugs, and blankets.

❖ **Bouclé** One or more thin, tightly spun yarns plied with a soft-spun thicker yarn. The softer yarn curls back on itself producing random loops.

❖ **Ribbon** Ribbons come in many different forms. They can be strips of woven fabric or a knitted tube. Use woven fabric ribbons for weaving and avoid the knitted ones because they can ravel when cut and stretch with use. Some woven-ribbon yarns don't work well as warp because they fray, but these can be used as weft.

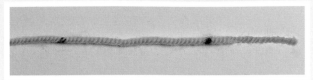

This is a knitting yarn, unstretched. The area between the two black dots is 2" long.

Helpful Tips
WEAVING VS KNITTING YARNS

I remember the first time that I, as a beginning weaver, wove a baby blanket. I wanted to use fine washable wool, so I chose a soft knitting yarn. I didn't realize how much elasticity was spun into this yarn and made no accommodation for it. When I wound the warp, I stretched the yarn so much that when it came off the warping board—surprise! I lost inches in length. Under tension on the loom, it stretched again, and it stretched even more as I wove. The more it stretched, the more tension I put on the warp. The selvedges pulled in due to the weft's elasticity, and when the blanket came off the loom, it rippled from all the various adjustments to tension I had made. I thought, oh well, wet-finishing should take care of this. Wrong again. The yarn was highly processed to make it a washable wool, and washing produced no change. Here's what I learned to do when I am using stretchy knitting yarns:

This is the same knitting yarn, stretched. The yarn increased in length by ¾".

COMBINING AND SUBSTITUTING YARNS

Because I weave mostly plain weave, I like to combine or substitute different types of yarn to create interesting fabrics. The key to success for combining and substituting yarns is to match fiber characteristics. Use protein-based fibers together (fibers made from animal hair or fur) or cellulose-based fibers together (fibers made from plant materials). Test for shrinkage differences. This is important for the weft yarns, too, because the fabric can finish with varying widths if the fibers stretch or wash differently.

1. Wind the warp with minimum tension on the warping board.

2. Beam the warp with minimum tension.

3. Weave with consistent, moderate tension (just enough to open a shed).

4. If the weft is the same type of yarn as the warp, allow consistent and ample ease (weft angle or arc); otherwise, you'll lose width when warp tension is removed.

5. Always sample first to determine whether or not a yarn will full during washing; many knitting yarns do not.

For learning how yarns behave during weaving, sewing, and finishing, experience is the best teacher.

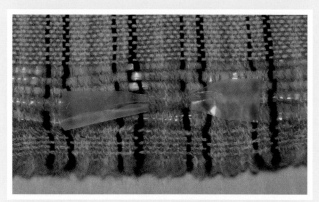

Thin strips of plastic used as waste yarn can remain in the fabric during wet-finishing and be removed when the fabric is dry.

USING WASTE YARN (WEFT FILLER)

Waste yarn is the weft used to spread the warp, to secure raw edges, to secure areas used for warp fringe, and to separate pieces during weaving. For projects with yarns that full during wet-finishing, I leave the waste yarn in during wet-finishing to keep the fringe from fulling and matting together. The waste yarn therefore needs to be smooth and nonfulling. I like to use 1" strips that I cut from plastic dry-cleaner bags. They're easy to pull out and reuse. Before washing, tie the warp fringe to hold the waste yarn in place at both raw edges.

CONES VS SKEINS

Yarn on a cone is very efficient to use for winding a warp or bobbins. The yarn feeds easily off the top of the cone and is usually abundant enough that you never need to cut and tie ends together. To use knitting and novelty yarns that come on skeins, you will want to use skein and ball winders. I recommend rewinding the ball of yarn after the first winding. The yarn will form the second ball with much less tension, making it easier to pull from its center without catching or tangling.

Whether you're working with cones or with skeins, there will be times when you run out of yarn or encounter a knot. If there is a knot in the warp yarn when you're winding the warp, end the yarn at the nearest beginning or ending peg, retie the yarn, and continue winding. If you encounter a knot in the weft while you are weaving or if you need to join a new yarn with one that is ending, splice them as described in Weaving Tips, page 93.

LOCAL YARN STORE (LYS) VS INTERNET

Having owned a yarn store for many years, I support local yarn stores as much as is practical. Local is what's local to me while I'm traveling, too. I enjoy visiting yarn stores in different parts of the country because each has a unique flavor and inventory. Some long-established stores that started out as weaving shops have added knitting, and I count on them to have a good selection of weaving yarns and lovely knitting novelties.

When I'm home and can't get the right yarn locally for a project, I do turn to the Internet. I usually order yarns I'm familiar with. Every computer screen has a different color calibration, and no matter how accurate colors are at the point of origin, what you see is going to be slightly different from the actual yarn. Order samples or color cards if you have the time for mail. This will save time later if a yarn arrives and it's not the right color or texture and you have to return it or look for a replacement. Of course, you can always add it to your stash!

For learning how yarns behave during weaving, sewing, and finishing, experience is the best teacher. Try different yarns and weave structures. Weave and wet-finish a lot of samples. You'll gain a feel for what adjustments to make for the effects you want. Winding the warp and threading the loom can tell you a lot about a yarn's elasticity and strength. You'll learn to use a more open reed when you need to avoid abrasion, sleying two ends in each dent instead of one, for example. Trying different setts and wet-finishing the samples can teach you how to give yarns room to full, how much to allow for shrinkage, and how to get the drape you want.

Ribbon Boa

DESIGN NOTES

Boas (narrow furry or feathery scarf-like accessories) are fun to make and can add flair to just about any item in your wardrobe. The feathery look can be achieved in a woven cloth by using yarns and/or ribbons as weft threads that extend beyond the selvedge ("side" fringes), providing an ideal role for novelty yarns of all types.

EQUIPMENT

2-shaft loom, 4-shaft loom, or rigid-heddle loom, 8" weaving width; 8 dent reed or rigid heddle; 2 shuttles (you'll need a stick shuttle for the ribbon yarn); tapestry needle.

MATERIALS

Warp Rayon chenille (100% viscose, 1,300 yd/lb, 2,625 m/kg, Silk City), Cayenne #743, 32 yd; Coventry #959, 28 yd. 2 strands monofilament, each 3" from the chenille selvedge on each side, 5 total yd.

Weft Rayon chenille, Cayenne #743, 20 yd. Ribbon (¾" wide, 100% polyamide, 120 yd/100 g skein, Segue, Trendsetter Yarn), Roses Are Red #1010, 80 yd.

Boas are very quick to weave—you can get one on and off the loom in just a few hours. Always remember to sample first because different yarns will behave, look, and drape differently in the side fringe. For this boa, I used a wide ribbon for the side fringe and left the weft loops, but the loops can also be cut. When you sample, try both ways before deciding on the final design.

When I wound the warp for this boa, I planned to weave three projects on the same warp—a boa, a collar, and a scarf (see also pages 20–27). The boa and collar use the same sett, but for the scarf, I opened the sett and spaced the warp (skipping dents) to allow the ribbon weft to show in the spaces and to produce a more scarf-like drape. The directions in this book are for a separate warp for each of these projects, but you can put on a long warp (5 yards or so), weave all three, and then also try other novelty yarns, different colors of ribbon, and/or varied fringe lengths for more pieces.

WARP MEASUREMENTS

Total warp ends 30 (see Warp Color Order).

Warp length 2 yd (allows for take-up and 27" loom waste).

SETTS

EPI 16 in the chenille core (2/dent in an 8-dent reed).

PPI 12.

FABRIC MEASUREMENTS

Width in reed 7⅞" (1⅞" for the chenille core band plus 1 strand monofilament 3" beyond each chenille selvedge; monofilament is removed later).

Finished width 6⅝" (1⅝" for core band plus 2½" ribbon-weft loops as fringe on each side).

Woven length (measured under tension on the loom) 42".

Finished length 46" (About 41" for the core band plus 2½" added ribbon-loop fringe at each end).

Take-up 10–12%.

Warp Color Order

	7x		
14		2	Coventry
16	2	2	Cayenne
30			

Weaving

Wind a warp of 30 ends following the Warp Color Order. Use your preferred method to warp the loom, sleying 2/dent in an 8-dent reed. The 30 chenille ends will weave the core band of the boa with the chenille weft. Note that chenille can break if pulled too tightly. For a way to tie the warp onto the front apron rod that can prevent stressing individual ends, see the Lashing Method for Tying On, page 90.

Tie 1 strand of monofilament to the front apron rod 3" from each selvedge (skip 24 dents for each), suspend from the back beam without threading in a heddle, and weight with a C-clamp or other weight. The (side-fringe) ribbon weft passes around the monofilament similarly to a floating selvedge.

Spread the warp by weaving plain weave with waste yarn in the chenille core section for about 3". To weave the boa, use 1 shuttle with Cayenne chenille and wind a stick shuttle with ribbon following the directions in Weaving with Ribbon, page 92.

Weave 2 picks of plain weave with Cayenne chenille in the core chenille section only. Place the ribbon in the next shed, leaving a weft tail of about 90" to use later for making a looped fringe along this raw edge. Then weave the boa fabric for 42", alternating 2 picks chenille in the chenille core section with 2 picks of ribbon, taking the ribbon around the monofilament on each side. When you are weaving with the chenille, take the chenille shuttle under the ribbon before passing it into the next shed to secure the ribbon at the core selvedge. Take care when you are inserting the ribbon not to pull in the monofilament, which would shorten the ribbon loops. When you weave the last pick of ribbon, leave about 90" of ribbon tail that will become the looped fringe at this raw edge. End with 2 picks of plain weave with chenille in the chenille core section only and then weave 3" in the core section using waste yarn. Remove the fabric from the loom. Pull out the monofilament from the weft loops.

Finishing

Working with one end of the boa at a time, remove the waste yarn and follow the steps in Looped Fringe for using the 90" tail to make the fringe at each end of the boa. Lightly steam the boa with a fabric steamer or an iron; see Seaming vs Pressing, page 120.

LOOPED FRINGE

1 Between each same-color pair of chenille warp threads, pull the length of ribbon into a loop that is the same length as the side-fringe loops (about 3" under tension).

2 Tie the 2 chenille ends in a tight overhand knot around the ribbon to secure it.

3 Trim the chenille tails close to the knot (to about ¼" beyond the knot).

4 The chenille knots are hidden by the ribbon fringe.

5 When all of the loops are tied securely, use a tapestry needle to weave the ribbon end into the chenille core.

Ribbon Collar

DESIGN NOTES

To use this idea for a collar and maximize the effect of the two fringes, I wove the side fringe for the collar in two lengths, one about 2" long, one about ¾" long. The collar is worn with the long fringe falling over the fabric band so that a bit of the fabric shows below the fringe, and the shorter fringe shows below that. If you use other yarns than the ribbon weft for this project, be sure to sample first since not all yarns will drape the same way.

The idea for this collar came when I was playing around with the sample I wove for the Ribbon Boa. I turned the sample on its side so that the ribbon fringe along one selvedge fell over the band. I'm intrigued with the idea of designing a collar like this for the neckline of a handwoven garment. Different yarns or ribbons will create very different looks.

EQUIPMENT

2-shaft loom, 4-shaft loom, or rigid-heddle loom, 6" weaving width; 8-dent reed or rigid heddle; 2 shuttles (you'll need a stick shuttle for the ribbon yarn), tapestry needle, 1 snap, 1 button (optional).

MATERIALS

Warp Rayon chenille (100% viscose, 1,300 yd/lb, 2,625 m/kg, Silk City), Cayenne #743, 24 yd; Coventry #959, 21 yd. 2 strands monfilament, one placed 1" from the chenille selvedge on one side, the other 2¼" from the chenille selvedge on the other side, 4 total yd.

Weft Rayon chenille, Cayenne #743, 12 yd. Ribbon (¾" wide, 100% polyamide, 120 yd/100 g skein, 550 yd/lb, 1,110 m/kg, Segue, Trendsetter Yarn), Roses Are Red #1010, 20 yd.

Other Matching sewing thread.

WARP MEASUREMENTS

Total warp ends 30 (see Warp Color Order).

Warp length 1½ yd (allows for take-up and 27" loom waste).

SETTS

EPI 16.
PPI 12.

FABRIC MEASUREMENTS

Width in reed 5⅛" (1⅞" for the core band plus 1 strand monofilment 1" away from the selvedge on the left side and 1 strand monofilament 2¼" away from the selvedge on the right side).

Finished width 4¼" (1⅝" for core band plus ¾" for the ribbon loops on the left side, 1⅞" ribbon loops for the fringe on the right side).

Woven length (measured under tension on the loom) 22½".

Finished length 21".

Take-up 10–12%.

Warp Color Order

	7x		
14	2		Coventry
16	2	2	Cayenne
30			

Weaving

Wind a warp of 30 ends following the Warp Color Order. Use your preferred method to warp the loom, sleying 2/dent in an 8-dent reed. These 30 ends will weave the core band of the collar with the chenille weft. Note that chenille can break if pulled too tightly. For a way to tie the warp onto the front apron rod that can prevent stressing individual ends, see the Lashing Method for Tying On, page 90.

The ribbon weft will pass around a strand of monofilament to extend beyond the chenille fabric: Tie 1 strand of monofilament to the front apron rod 1" from the left selvedge (skip 8 dents) and a 2nd strand 2¼" away from the right selvedge (skip 18 dents), suspend them from the back beam without threading in a heddle, and weight each with a C-clamp or other weight.

Spread the warp with waste yarn by weaving plain weave in the chenille section only for 3". To weave the collar, use 1 shuttle for the Cayenne chenille weft and wind a stick shuttle with ribbon (see Weaving with Ribbon, page 92). Weave 1¾" plain weave with chenille in the chenille section only.

Place the ribbon after tapering the end into the next shed with the tapered tail extending for about 1½" to secure into the following ribbon shed. To weave the band, alternate 1 pick chenille in the chenille core only with 1 pick of ribbon, taking the ribbon around the monofilament on alternate sides. When you are weaving with the chenille, take the chenille shuttle under the ribbon before passing it into the next shed to secure the ribbon at the selvedge. Make sure when you are inserting the ribbon not to draw in the monofilament, which would shorten the ribbon loops. Continue to alternate shuttles every 2 picks until the woven piece measures 19". End with 1¾" plain weave using chenille in the chenille core section only, and then weave 3" with waste yarn. Remove the fabric from the loom. Pull out the monofilament from the weft loops.

Finishing

Remove the waste yarn and needleweave the chenille warp threads back into the body of the cloth. Trim tails flush with the fabric. Sew the male side of the snap on the wrong side of one end of the collar.

Position the collar ends so they overlap at right angles and sew the female side of the snap on the right side of the collar end; the collar will form a V at the closure (see Finishing the Collar). Lightly steam the collar using a fabric steamer or an iron (see Steaming vs Pressing, page 120). If you have a dress form, steam the collar directly on the form so that the longer ribbon falls down on top of the chenille band.

You can add a button to the top of the closure or leave it plain. I wanted to enhance the elegance of the collar, so I chose a vintage velvet and beaded button as just the right addition (see Buttons, pages 123–124).

FINISHING THE COLLAR

1 For each warp thread: thread the end into a tapestry needle and needleweave alongside an adjacent warp thread for about ¾".

2 Continue weaving in each thread.

3 Clip the warp tails close to the fabric.

4 The warp threads are woven in and now invisible.

5 Sew snaps on the ends of the collar; male on wrong side of top end and female on right side of bottom end.

6 Finished collar with ends overlapped and snapped to close.

Ribbon Scarf

To create the Ribbon Scarf, I used a more open sett than for the Boa and Collar and skipped dents to create spaces. Ribbon is used as the only weft in the scarf, not a combination of ribbon and chenille as in the others. The ribbon pops out in the open spaces, and both the looser sett and the soft texture of the ribbon weft provide a drapable fabric suitable for scarves or shawls.

DESIGN NOTES

If you want to weave all three projects on the same warp as I did (Ribbon Collar, Ribbon Boa, Ribbon Scarf), add two yards to the warp length given in these instructions. For wider scarves or shawls, add to warp width by adding repeats to the Warp Color Order; add to warp length for a longer piece or more than one. The warping and weaving go so quickly that you can easily weave several scarves in just a few hours.

EQUIPMENT

2-shaft loom, 4-shaft loom, or rigid-heddle loom, 6" weaving width; 8-dent reed or rigid heddle; 2 shuttles (you'll need a stick shuttle for the ribbon yarn).

MATERIALS

Warp Rayon chenille (100% viscose, 1,300 yd/lb, 2,620 m/kg, Silk City), Cayenne #743, 44 yd; Coventry #959, 39 yd.

Weft Rayon chenille (100% viscose, 1,300 yd/lb, Silk City), # Cayenne #743, 5 yd. Ribbon (¾" wide, 100% polyamide, 120 yd/100 g skein, 550 yd/lb, 1,110 m/kg, Segue, Trendsetter Yarn), Fall Leaves #501, 85 yd.

WARP MEASUREMENTS

Total warp ends 30 (see Warp Color Order).

Warp length 2¾ yd (allows for take-up and 27" loom waste).

SETTS

EPI 5¾ (6 ends at 1/dent in an 8-dent reed alternating with 3 empty dents).

PPI 8.

FABRIC MEASUREMENTS

Width in reed 5¼".

Finished width 4½".

Woven length (measured under tension on the loom) 60" for scarf body plus 6" waste-yarn sections at each end.

Finished length 58" plus 4" twisted fringe.

Take-up 12%.

Warp Color Order

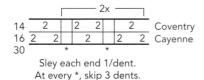

			2x		
14	2	2	2	2	Coventry
16	2	2	2	2	2	Cayenne
30		*		*	

Sley each end 1/dent.
At every *, skip 3 dents.

Weaving

Wind a warp of 30 ends following the Warp Color Order. Use your preferred method to warp the loom for plain weave, sleying the ends as shown in the Warp Color Order; note the skipped dents. Chenille yarn can break if pulled too tightly. For a way to tie the warp onto the front apron rod that can prevent stressing individual ends, see the Lashing Method for Tying On, page 90.

Spread the warp with plain weave using waste yarn for about 6" (you'll need 6" of warp length for a final twisted fringe of 4"). Use 1 shuttle for the Cayenne chenille weft and wind a stick shuttle with ribbon (see Weaving with Ribbon, page 92. Weave 9 picks with chenille. Weave 59" in plain weave with the ribbon weft, tapering the ribbon ends to start and end the weft as described in Weaving with Ribbon. Weave 9 picks with chenille. Weave 6" with waste yarn and remove the fabric from the loom.

Finishing

Lightly steam the piece with a fabric steamer or an iron (see Steaming vs Pressing page 120). Remove the waste yarn just before preparing the twisted fringe on each end. (A twisted fringe can help control chenille's tendency to fray and tangle, and the contrast between the velvety chenille and the ribbon twists makes this fringe especially attractive.)

Make a twisted fringe of each stripe of 2 chenille ends: Twist the 2 ends separately in one direction as tightly as you can (chenille is slippery and needs to be extra tight for the fringe to hold). Then twist the 2 ends together in the opposite direction and secure with an overhand knot. For the ribbon fringes added between chenille fringes, see Twisted Ribbon Fringe.

TWISTED RIBBON FRINGE

1 Add ribbon to the fringe by taking 1 strand of ribbon through each space created by the empty dents just above the 9 picks of chenille and position the 2 ends of the strand together so they are equal in length. Twist the 2 ends separately in the same direction until they are very tight.

2 Bring the 2 twisted ends together.

3 Twist the 2 ends together in the opposite direction.

4 Secure with an overhand knot.

Monet Möbius

DESIGN NOTES

I had originally intended for this fabric to be a shawl, but somehow a shawl didn't seem special enough for it. It sat around the studio for a month, and then, while I was playing around with draping it, I wrapped it into a Möbius and saw right away that a Möbius was what it was meant to be. This experience reinforces a valuable lesson I learned during my draping class in college—my professor advised us to let the fabric "hang out" for awhile to see what shape works best for it. Don't force a cloth into something that works against its natural tendencies.

Wear this wrap around your head and shoulders or around your neck with the edge turned back into a collar. Place the seam at the bottom of the twist because that's where its natural weight occurs—it will be hidden there, too.

A chenille wrap is sumptuous to wear! It drapes beautifully, and the smooth, velvety texture of chenille provides an exquisitely soft hand. The Möbius shape takes special advantage of the natural drape of a chenille fabric.

In choosing and arranging the colors of the chenille in the warp, I wanted to emulate the watery effect of the wide ribbon I used as an accent warp thread between the chenille stripes. I discovered by sampling that blending colors in some of the stripes gives the fabric a shimmering quality, whereas using a single color in every stripe does not produce the same effect. That's why sampling is so important—you can test out various color and striping options to "preview" your cloth.

EQUIPMENT
2-shaft or 4-shaft loom, 23" weaving width; 8-dent reed; 2 shuttles.

MATERIALS
Warp Rayon chenille (100% viscose, 1,300 yd/lb, 2,625 m/kg, Silk City), Dark Navy #011, 330 yd; Blue Velvet, #232, 385 yd; Juniper #940, 154 yd. Ribbon (¾" wide, 100% polyamide, 120 yd/100 g

skein, 550 yd/lb, 1,110 m/kg, Segue, Trendsetter Yarn), Patchwork #1713, 55 yd.

Weft Rayon chenille, Dark Navy #011 and Blue Velvet #232, 180 yd each.

Other Navy sewing thread.

WARP MEASUREMENTS

Total warp ends 336 (see Warp Color Order).

Warp length 2¾ yd (allows for take-up, shrinkage, and 27" loom waste).

SETTS

EPI 16 for chenille (2/dent in an 8-dent reed); 8 for ribbon (1/dent).

PPI 8.

FABRIC MEASUREMENTS

Width in reed 22¼".

Width after washing 19½".

Woven length (measured under tension on the loom) 66".

Length after washing 62".

Length after sewing 60" (Möbius circumference).

Take-up and shrinkage 13% in width, 8% in length.

Warp Color Order

		4x		4x			4x							4x		4x				4x		4x			
20	1		1		1	1		1	1	1	1	1		1		1	1	1		1		1	1		ribbon
56							2		2	12			12		2		2								Juniper chenille
140			2		2	16	16	2		2			12		2		2	16	16	2		2			Blue Velvet chenille
120	16	16	2		2					12		12								2		2	16	16	Dark Navy chenille
336																									

Weaving

Wind a warp of 336 ends following the Warp Color Order. Use your preferred method to warp the loom for plain weave, sleying the chenille 2/dent and the ribbon 1/dent in an 8-dent reed and centering for 22¼". Note that chenille can break if pulled too tightly. For a way to tie the warp onto the front apron rod that can prevent stressing individual ends, see the Lashing Method for Tying On, page 90.

Spread the warp by weaving a header with waste yarn. Because the Möbius design does not include fringe, you can start weaving the fabric as soon as the warp is sufficiently spread. Using 1 shuttle with Dark Navy chenille and 1 shuttle with Blue Velvet chenille, weave plain weave at 8 ppi alternating 2 picks of each color until the chenille fabric measures 66". End with about ½" in waste yarn to secure the edge and then remove the fabric from the loom.

Washing

The chenille fabric may feel a bit stiff at this point. Don't be concerned! The magic happens during the washing process. Secure the raw edges with machine zigzagging just inside the waste-yarn picks, remove the waste yarn, and trim along the machine zigzagging.

Machine wash with a mild detergent on a gentle cycle in warm water with a warm rinse for about 20 minutes (note that this amount of agitation works with my front-loading washer; make adjustments for your machine; see Washing, pages 118–119). Lay flat to dry. Steam with a fabric steamer or an iron (see Steaming vs Pressing, page 120).

Assembly and Sewing

Lay the fabric on a flat surface and flip one zigzagged end completely over to make a full twist in the fabric. Use a concealed seam, also known as a flat-fell seam, to connect the two raw edges.

SEWING A FLAT-FELL SEAM

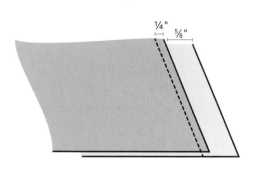

1 With the wrong sides of the fabric together (it's reversible so you decide which is which), take one zigzagged edge and line it up ⅝" short of the opposite edge, match the stripes, and pin together. Machine sew a seam ¼" from the short edge. Two seam allowances are made, one that is ¼" and one that is ⅝".

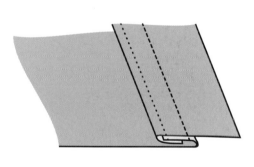

2 Fold the ⅝" seam allowance around the ¼" seam allowance to enclose it. Turn and flatten the fold against the fabric as for a hem and pin in place. Using sewing thread and a blind stitch, handsew the folded seam allowance close to the fold. Steam the seam the same way as you did the fabric.

Saori Belts

DESIGN NOTES

The designs and colors in these belts all happened spontaneously. I had leftover space-dyed ribbon from the Ribbon Collar that I used as a starting point for selecting weft yarns from my stash. I was especially attracted to bumpy rayons, velvety chenille, and fuzzy mohairs for their contrasting textures. Woven in a sturdy, weft-faced plain weave, these yarns will all wear well in a belt. If you don't have a focal yarn to inspire your color choices, pull yarns based on color families and go from there. The lengths of yarns you'll use are so short that if a yarn doesn't work well, you can easily pull it out and try something else.

I must caution you—making these belts is addictive! I call them Saori for the free-style way they are woven; Saori is a method of weaving established in the 1960s by Misao Jo that celebrates the spontaneous use of weft yarns and colors. Working intimately with so many ever-changing yarns and colors is so appealing that you can't stop with just one belt. So I suggest you warp the loom for several, gather yarns from your stash, and get started on a colorful, rewarding journey (amounts given here are for one belt; allow a little more than a yard of warp length for each additional belt).

EQUIPMENT

2-shaft loom, 4-shaft loom, or rigid-heddle loom, 4" weaving width; 6-dent reed or rigid heddle; several bobbins (optional); tapestry needle.

MATERIALS

Warp 8/4 unmercerized cotton (1,600 yd/lb, 3,230 m/kg, Cotton Carpet Warp, Maysville), Black #2, 52 yd.

Weft 8/4 unmercerized cotton, Black #2. A selection of yarns based on color families, textures, and weight, about 125 yd total per belt.

Other Three large hook-and-eye closures; black sewing thread; optional beads.

Color Options

Wind bobbins or butterflies (see Making a Yarn Butterfly, page 92) for all the weft yarns you plan to use. Having them ready will make the weaving go faster because you can quickly choose a yarn and keep weaving.

For each belt, use a variety of the different effects that can be achieved using color with weft-faced weaves:

❖ **One-color stripe** Using one color only, weave from selvedge to selvedge, beating firmly for a weft-faced cloth. Vary the stripe widths from ¼" to 1".

❖ **Narrow horizontal lines** that become vertical when worn: Using two colors, weave 2 picks of one color, then 2 picks of the second. Repeat this sequence for desired length.

❖ **Columns or vertical lines** that become horizontal when worn: Using two colors, weave 1 pick with one color, change sheds, then weave 1 pick of the second color. Repeat these 2 picks for desired length. For this, cross one color (shuttle) over or under the other between picks to interlock the wefts at the selvedges.

❖ **Two colors side by side** Both colors are woven in a section of the warp. One color passes from one selvedge and turns around a warp thread in the center of the warp and then returns to the selvedge in the next plain-weave shed. Using the same two sheds, the other color passes from the opposite selvedge and turns around the same warp thread in the center to return to the opposite selvedge in the next plain-weave shed. Continue alternating 2 picks of each color until your color blocks are the desired height.

Weaving

Wind a warp of 26 ends of 8/4 cotton. Use your preferred method to warp the loom for plain weave, sleying 1/dent in a 6-dent reed (sley the first and last pair of ends 2/dent but thread in separate heddles); center for 4". Tie the warp onto the front apron rod.

Spread the warp by weaving a 1" header using waste yarn or until the warp is evenly spread. Weave 6 picks with 8/4 cotton as an edging, beating firmly. Then start weaving the belt, changing the wefts and color

WARP MEASUREMENTS

Total warp ends 26.

Warp length 2 yd (allows for take-up, shrinkage, and 34" loom waste).

SETTS

EPI 6.
PPI 20–30 (varies based on yarn used).

FABRIC MEASUREMENTS

Width in reed 4".

Width after washing 3½".

Woven length (measured under tension on the loom) 34" (for a finished belt that is 32" around the waist). You can weave the belt longer than the desired finished length and then remove weft picks to fit your waist.

Length after sewing About ½" shorter than relaxed length off loom (needleweaving the ends back into the edges tightens the edges about that much).

Take-up About 5% in width and length.

orders as described above. The warp tends to show in the most recent picks you make, but as you continue to weave, the prior picks will pack in and the warp will be covered.

Work until the belt is the desired length under tension. Place a thread marker every 10" to keep accurate track of the measured length. When you remove the belt from the loom, it will continue to relax a bit more to become slightly shorter, so allow about 1" for this (i.e., weave the belt 2" longer than the desired finished length: the belt will lose about an inch in length when you release the tension and another inch as it continues to relax off the loom). End with 6 picks of 8/4 cotton, beating firmly. Weave about ½" with waste yarn to secure the ends and remove the belt from the loom, allowing about 4" unwoven warp beyond the waste yarn.

Finishing

Remove all the waste yarn from each end. With a tapestry needle, needleweave each warp thread back into the path of the adjacent warp thread for about 1". Trim the excess tails after all ends are woven in. Using black sewing thread, evenly space 3 hooks and corresponding eyes on the back of each end of the belt and sew in place. Place optional beads along the edges of both ends, spacing them as you like, and sew in place.

FINISHING THE BELTS

1 Trim the tails close to the fabric.

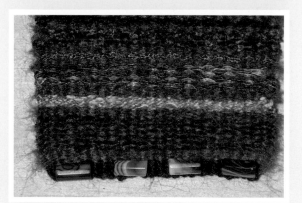

2 Sew beads on the edges of both ends.

CHAPTER 3

Drape

When we talk about the elements that contribute to the "drape" of a handwoven fabric, yarn, weave structure, and finishing methods all have to be considered—all three play an important role.

We talk subjectively about the "hand" and feel of a fabric. We do the "weaver's handshake" when we greet fellow weavers—rubbing their cloth between our thumb and index finger and remarking how the fabric feels to the touch. In school, I was taught how to drape a fabric by letting the cloth dictate what shape it was best suited for.

Whatever term you use—drape, feel, or hand—it is a way of describing a fabric's flexibility (is it pliable or stiff), resiliency (does it accommodate movement, does it maintain its shape without wrinkling), density (determined by sett and weave structure), and overall texture (is it rough or smooth, silky or matte).

To determine sett for a yarn, wrap a ruler or gauge for 1".

Harrisville Shetland wool in a balanced plain weave at 12 epi and 12 ppi, hung on the bias.

Harrisville Shetland wool in a balanced plain weave at 6 epi and 6 ppi, hung on the bias.

Draping qualities also depend on how a fabric is cut and then constructed, whether on the bias or with the warp running vertically or horizontally. The most drape usually comes from a bias-cut fabric, but cutting pieces on the diagonal wastes cloth, and for weavers cloth is too precious to waste.

Setts and Weave Structures

The term "sett" refers to the number of warp ends and weft picks per inch used to weave a fabric. To determine the sett for projects in plain weave, wind the warp yarn around a ruler for 1", being careful not to stretch the yarn, overlap the wraps, or leave gaps between them. Then count the number of wraps. For a balanced plain weave (the same number of ends per inch as picks per inch), divide this number by 2 to get

the number of warp ends and weft picks per inch. If you're mixing yarns in the warp, wrap the ruler using each yarn in proportion to its use in the final cloth. You may want to wind more than 1" to get an average of all the yarns.

On either end of the balanced plain-weave spectrum are warp-faced weaves and weft-faced weaves. In a warp-faced fabric, the weft doesn't show; in a weft-faced fabric, the warp doesn't show. Both weaves are usually dense and relatively stiff—suitable for mats and rugs. The weft-faced structure in the Saori Belts, for example, produces the sturdy hand appropriate for a belt.

Warp and weft sett greatly affect drape. The two photos above show samples of Harrisville Shetland wool (1,800 yd/lb) woven in balanced plain weave at 12 epi/ppi (left sample) and 6 epi/ppi (right sample).

Plain-weave sample before washing, 10 epi, 10 ppi; after washing 12 epi, 12 ppi.

Twill sample before washing, 10 epi, 12 ppi; after washing, 13 epi; 14 ppi.

Striped Ruana, pages 44–49.

Both samples were the same size on the loom, 16½" square. Shrinkage after wet-finishing was 10% for the 12 epi/ppi sample but 16% for the 6 epi/ppi sample, and the 6 epi/ppi sample has considerably more drape.

The best way to determine sett, of course, is to sample. The two photos above each show a different weave structure woven in Harrisville Shetland wool; one is a balanced plain weave, the other a nearly balanced twill. Twills usually produce a denser fabric than plain weave—fewer interlacements allow closer setts. Both of these samples were the same size on the loom and were wet-finished the same way.

Sample!

If you use the yarn recommended for a published project and follow the project instructions exactly, you can get by without sampling. But all other times, unless you have woven with the same yarn and weave structure before and were pleased with the results, sample. Finding out what works before you warp and weave will cost less in time and money than weaving something that isn't right.

Project instructions in this book specify exactly the warp length required for the project, including take-up and loom waste. Consider adding to this length for sampling or weaving two projects instead of one. It won't take that much extra time, and you may discover new ideas to apply to the second piece. Save and use your thrums for future projects—boas, rya knots, stuffing, or embellishments.

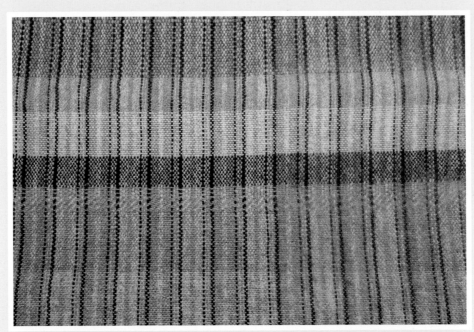

This sample shows different weft yarns (mohair and wool) and colors (black, cream, taupe) for the Striped Ruana; the right half of sample is brushed; the left half is not brushed.

Make your sample at least 6" wide; wider is even better. I like to judge the drape of a sample, so most of mine are 10" wide or wider. Make the warp long enough to allow for cutting off samples, resleying the reed, and retying on, if necessary (1½ to 2 yards long plus loom waste). (See Weaving Tips, page 91, for a quick way to retie the warp to the apron rod.)

Sampling informs us. You can determine how the yarn reacts through the whole warping and weaving process and make changes as needed—replacing snarly, sticky, or weak yarns or figuring out how to accommodate them; changing warp setts; changing the beat; and more.

Try out various weft yarns and colors. This is very important when you are weaving a sample for a garment. For the Striped Ruana, I wove a large sample—19" wide by 14" long (see the photo above). I tested a roving weft (at the top of the sample), a

mohair weft (the next weft in the sample), and a number of different weft colors, and I wove both plain weave and twill. I brushed the right half of the sample and left the other half unbrushed. I studied the sample from a distance so I could see which weft color integrated best with the warp. The cream weft made the black warp pop out too much; the black weft overpowered all the other colors. The brushing toned down the colors and striping.

You can cut a large sample apart and wet-finish each section differently to see how each method affects shrinkage, fulls the yarns, or causes dyes to run. You can also use the samples to try out different techniques for edging, sewing, trims, and embellishments.

Label your samples, learn from them, save them, and use the information gained for future projects.

Striped Mohair Shawl

DESIGN NOTES

This mohair blend creates a lightweight fabric and is very warm—the perfect wrap for traveling. It's very practical, too. It has great drape, so it can be worn as a shawl or a scarf (as shown here) or wrapped multiple times around the neck. You can fold it into a 6" by 9" rectangle, place it in a Ziploc bag, squeeze the air out, and carry it anywhere. It can be dressy or casual—truly the perfect travel item!

I wove both this shawl and the Plaid Cowl on the same warp, though these instructions are for only the shawl. If you want to weave multiple projects on the same warp, remember to add additional length between pieces to accommodate fringing or other finishing methods.

I like to travel light. You may wonder what that has to do with this shawl! Recently, I was unexpectedly stuck in the Mexico City airport overnight. The doors were wide open to the night air, and I became extremely chilled. Fortunately, I had my hat, gloves, and a sweater in my carry-on, but I didn't have a shawl to wrap around my neck and shoulders. Hence, I was inspired to weave one.

EQUIPMENT

2-shaft loom, 4-shaft loom, or rigid-heddle loom, 23" weaving width; 10-dent reed or rigid heddle; 1 shuttle.

MATERIALS

Warp Kid mohair/nylon blend (70% kid mohair, 30% nylon, 4,450 yd/lb, 8,980 m/kg, Kid Mohair Lace Weight, Louet), Dark Olive #41, 285 yd; Silver #38, 270 yd.

Weft Kid mohair/nylon blend, Silver #38, 485 yd.

WARP MEASUREMENTS

Total warp ends 222 (see Warp Color Order).

Warp length 2½ yd (allows for take-up, shrinkage, and 25" loom waste).

SETTS

EPI 10.
PPI 10.

FABRIC MEASUREMENTS

Width in reed 22⅕."

Width after washing 20".

Woven length (measured under tension on the loom) 67".

Length after washing 62" plus 1¼" fringe at each end.

Take-up and shrinkage 10–12% in width and length.

Warp Color Order

		⌈27x⌉		
108		4		Dark Olive
114	1	4	5	Silver
222				

Weaving

Wind a warp of 222 ends following the Warp Color Order. Use your preferred method to warp the loom for plain weave. However, if you warp front to back, raise shafts 1 and 3 on a 4-shaft loom, shaft 2 on a 2-shaft loom, or the heddle on the rigid-heddle loom while you are beaming the warp. Separating the threads from each other will help prevent the warp threads from sticking to each other.

Spread the warp by weaving plain weave using a smooth nonfulling waste yarn (see Using Waste Yarn, page 15) for about 3". With the Silver Kid Mohair weft, begin weaving the shawl in plain weave, beating the first 6 picks firmly in place (almost weft-faced) to secure the raw edge. Continue weaving, beating lightly to obtain a balanced weave (10 ppi). To prevent the mohair yarns from sticking to each other, when you are changing sheds using a 4-shaft loom, raise the shafts individually—use a direct tie-up to do this. For instance, raise shaft 1, then 3, then throw the shuttle. Raise shaft 2, then 4, then throw the shuttle. Once the cloth starts to wrap around the cloth beam, start winding packing paper with the cloth to keep the layers separated from the tie-on knots and prevent them from distorting the cloth.

Continue weaving until the fabric measures 66"; end by beating the last 6 picks firmly as at the beginning. Weave 3" with waste yarn and remove the fabric from the loom allowing enough warp length beyond the waste-yarn sections to tie loose knots.

Washing

Tie knots in the warp threads at both ends of the shawl to secure the waste yarn during washing (this will keep the fringes from getting tangled and matted). Machine wash with a mild detergent on a gentle cycle in warm water with a warm rinse for about 20 minutes (note that this amount of agitation works with my front-loading washer; make adjustments for your machine; see Washing, pages 118–119). Lay flat to dry. Remove the waste yarn and then steam using a fabric steamer or an iron (see Steaming vs Pressing, page 120).

Finishing

For an unknotted fringe, using a nylon-bristle brush, brush the raw edges away from the fringe in the warp direction to secure the last 6 picks. Then brush the entire cloth in the direction of the warp. You will get some slight shifting of the weft, but that's okay. Don't be too aggressive with the brushing—just enough to raise the "halo" of the mohair. You may want to lightly steam each section as you brush it to help raise the nap. When you have finished brushing, comb out the fringe to straighten (a wide-toothed comb makes this easier to do). You can decide if you want a short or long fringe. I chose to make the fringe on this shawl short, about 1¼", to limit the tangling or catching of the sticky mohair during use.

BRUSHING

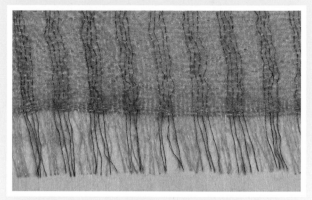

1 The first and last 6 picks at the ends are brushed toward the woven fabric. Because the mohair is sticky, there's no need to secure the fringe any other way.

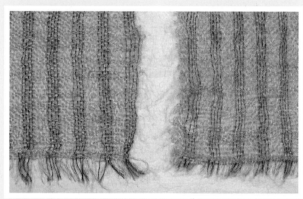

2 Brushed mohair sample (right) and unbrushed mohair sample (left). Both have been washed the same way. The brushed sample shows more halo and the stripes are more muted because of the raising of the nap.

Striped Ruana

I have a ruana that's about thirty years old. I've worn it plenty, so it's looking shabby. Because ponchos and ruanas have made a comeback in fashion, I decided it was time to weave an updated version. In the design for this one, slits are strategically placed in the waist area so the poncho can be worn with a belt—or not!

The inspiration to "frame" the piece with an edging came from the lovely tubular edgings of contemporary Peruvian ponchos. Although I might be able to make a tubular edging with much trial and error, I opted for knitting a wider, more flexible edging. Knitting such a long strip is tedious—very tedious—but it helped me catch up on a favorite TV series. The edging does indeed frame the striped pattern in the poncho, making it stand out—just as a frame does for a painting.

DESIGN NOTE

This ruana can be woven with a seam down the center back (as described here) or, if you have a wide loom, you can weave the back in one piece and weave the fronts side by side with two shuttles.

EQUIPMENT

2-shaft or 4-shaft loom, 22" weaving width; 15-dent reed; 2 shuttles; tapestry needle; size 4 (3.5 mm) knitting needles.

MATERIALS

Warp 2-ply wool, (1,800 yd/lb, 3,630 m/kg, Harrisville Shetland, Harrisville Designs), Suede #47, 741 yd; Ebony #85, 258 yd; Silver Mist #53, 714 yd.

Weft 2-ply wool, Suede #47, 1,290 yd.

Other 2-ply wool, Suede #47, 350 yd for 8½ yd of knitted edging. Sewing thread to match Suede.

WARP MEASUREMENTS

Total warp ends 326 (see Warp Color Order).

Warp length 5¼ yd (allows for take-up, shrinkage, and 27" loom waste).

SETTS

EPI 15.
PPI 12.

FABRIC MEASUREMENTS

Width in reed 21¾".

Width after washing 19".

Woven length (measured under tension on the loom) 160" (1½" waste-yarn section, 77" first panel, 3" waste-yarn section, 77" second panel, 1½" waste-yarn section).

Length after washing 143" (1¼" waste-yarn section, 69" first panel, 2½" waste-yarn section, 69" second panel, 1¼" waste-yarn section).

Length after sewing 70½" for each of the two panels after attaching edging.

Take-up and shrinkage 10% in width and length.

Weaving

Before winding the warp, make sure you have sampled and followed the instructions for measuring and making a muslin (see Making a Sample Garment, pages 58–59). Make any adjustments needed to warp width and length.

Wind a warp of 326 ends following the Warp Color Order. Use your preferred method to warp the loom for plain weave, sleying 1/dent in a 15-dent reed and centering for 21¾". Tie the warp onto the front apron rod.

Spread the warp by weaving a 1½" header using a smooth, nonfulling waste yarn (see Using Waste Yarn, page 15); add to header size if you want a fringed bottom edge.

The ruana is woven in two panels that are sewn together with a center-back seam (leaving the fronts open). To make measuring the woven panels easier, mark every 10" with a thread along the selvedge as you weave so you can keep track of the length of each panel. Also place a thread at the selvedge when you begin and end the belt slits (when you are matching the panels, these marker threads will help you align the two pieces for seaming).

When you end one weft and begin another, wet splice the joins (see Wet Splicing, page 93) for a smooth transition.

Weave plain weave with Suede wool weft until the fabric measures 13½". Mark the center 2 warp threads by looping a piece of sewing thread around them, and now using 2 shuttles, weave with 1 shuttle on each side, leaving a 3" slit for a belt opening between these 2 warp threads (see Weaving a Slit, page 91).

Warp Color Order

						7x									
136	3	1	1	5	5	1	1	3	1	1	5	5	1	1	Silver Mist
49	1		2		1		2		1		2		1		2		1	Ebony
141	5	5	1	1	3	1	1	5	5	1	1	3	1	1	5	Suede
326															

Be careful to maintain the same ppi (12) when you are weaving with 2 shuttles as you did with 1 shuttle.

After the slit measures 3", temporarily sew it closed using a cotton thread. The thread will be removed after the fabric is washed. (Sewing it closed will help avoid any gaps in the web above the opening.) Resume weaving with 1 shuttle for another 44". Weave another 3" slit in the same way as before. When the slit is complete and sewn closed, weave 13½"; end the panel by weaving 3" in plain weave with waste yarn.

Weave the second panel exactly as the first (not including the waste-yarn section at the start), ending with 1½" in waste yarn to secure the edge and then remove the fabric from the loom allowing enough warp length (about 4" at each end) to tie loose knots.

Washing

Tie loose knots in the warp at each end to secure the waste yarn and machine wash with a mild detergent on a gentle cycle in warm water with warm rinse for about 28 minutes (note that this amount of agitation works with my front-loading washer; make adjustments for your machine; see Washing, pages 118–119). Lay flat to dry. Remove waste yarn and trim fringe to a bit more than the desired final length if you'd like a fringed edge; otherwise trim to about 1". Steam using a fabric steamer or an iron (see Steaming vs Pressing, page 120). Cut the two panels apart. Remove the temporary cotton thread from the belt openings.

Sewing

Machine zigzag the ends of each panel (unless you opt to have a fringed-bottom edging) and trim to the zigzagging (see Machine Zigzagging, page 120). The zigzagging will be hidden in the edging.

Lay the two panels next to each other so that the striping sequences mirror each other, joining the two selvedges that each have a single Ebony wool edge warp thread. Pin the back seam from the hemline for 32" and try on the ruana, making sure it hangs evenly on the front and back of your body; adjust the length of the seam if necessary. Using a tapestry needle and Suede wool, sew the back seam using an invisible stitch (see Invisible Joining Stitch, page 120).

Finishing

Using a nylon-bristle brush, brush the fabric in the direction of the warp to raise the nap (see Brushing, pages 119–120). This is easier to do right after the fabric is steamed (steam a section, brush, steam a section, brush). Do this on both sides of the fabric. If you opt to have a fringed edge, brush the bottom raw edge away from the fringe to secure the last picks; trim the fringe to the desired length and then brush it, too.

KNIT EDGING

The edging is knitted separately, washed by hand, and then sewn onto the ruana. (Washing the edging gives it the same fulled texture as the fabric.) Using a cotton waste yarn and size 4 knitting needle, cast on 6 stitches with a temporary cast-on that will be removed later. Change to Suede wool and knit in stockinette stitch until the knitted strip is long enough to cover all the edges of the ruana (about 8½ yd for this one).

FINISHING DETAILS

1 Machine zigzag the bottom edges of each panel.

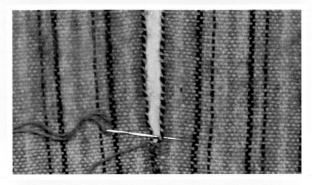

2 Sew two panels together using an invisible stitch.

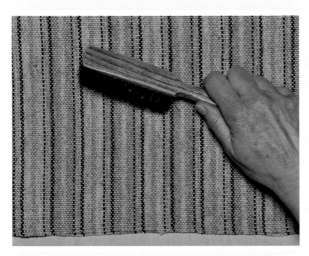

3 Using a nylon-bristle brush, brush the fabric warpwise.

4 Knit the edging.

5 Attach the edging to the panel.

The invisible stitch joins the panels; the ends of the knit edging are joined with the Kitchener stitch.

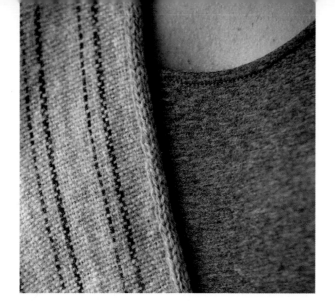

PLANNING STRIPES

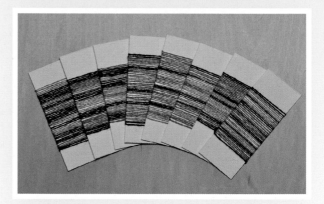

Do not bind off the wool; work ½" in cotton waste yarn and slip a pin through the open stitches in case you need to add more rows to the edging. Wash by hand in warm water, with a mild detergent and a warm rinse; lay flat to dry.

Starting at the top of the center back seam with right sides together, sew one side of the knitted edging to the edge of the right side of one front, not including the first cotton stitches. Using a tapestry needle and Suede wool, invisibly stitch into the space between the outside and the next row of stitches on the edging and into the fabric 3 warp ends in from the selvedge edges and just above the zigzagging on the raw edges until the knitted edging is sewn to all edges of the ruana. Make sure the fabric and edging remain smooth without rippling and allow ease in the edging around the corners. If you run out of edging, remove the cotton waste yarn at the end and knit more edging (wash the added section by hand). When you reach the top edge of the center back seam where you started, remove the cotton waste yarn and work a stitch-to-stitch join, such as the Kitchener stitch, joining the two open ends of the edging.

Now wrap the knitted edging around the edges of the fabric, pin, and then sew on the wrong side of the ruana with invisible stitches about 3 warp threads from the selvedge edges and completely covering the zigzagged raw edges.

Steam the final edging and the ruana.

To plan the warp for the Striped Ruana, I wound many variations of the warp colors, some lighter in value, some darker.

After I had a sequence I liked, I counted the number of threads in the stripe repeat and divided that into the number of warp threads I needed for the warp width to determine how many repeats of the stripe sequence to thread. Because the repeat did not divide evenly, I had to modify the stripes by a thread or two. The tricky thing with this ruana was also planning the striping pattern so it would not call attention to the back seam and would provide a pleasing flow in the repeat of the stripes when the two panels were sewn together.

After making this adjustment, I began sampling (see page 39). The ruana is a large garment, and the striping was purposefully subtle. I didn't want it to scream, "Hi, I'm a big striped fabric." After the sample was washed, I hung it so I could see what the stripes looked like from a distance with the interplay of the weft. Did one weft color dull the striping more than another—particularly with the brushing? All of these steps determined the striping and finishing before I even started to weave the piece. Success!

Southwest Wrap

DESIGN NOTES

I am a firm believer in the importance of sampling, and for this wrap, the sampling had an unexpected serendipity. I threaded various stripe widths in the sample warp and experimented with different setts (20, 30, and 40 epi). The serendipity came with wet-finishing—the change in drape provided by the different setts inspired me to combine them in the final fabric. Because Tencel is slippery, the denser warp stripes (40 epi) are placed across the shoulder and neck area to give the fabric stability where the greatest stress occurs. The most open sett (20 epi) is worn across the bottom, producing a very slight ruffling of the fabric.

EQUIPMENT
2-shaft or 4-shaft loom, 37" weaving width; 10-dent reed; 4 shuttles.

MATERIALS

Warp 8/2 Tencel (100% lyocell, 3,360 yd/lb, 6,780 m/kg, Valley Yarns, WEBS), Gray Mauve, 974 yd; Deep Coral, 968 yd; Taupe 968 yd.

Weft 2-ply silk (1,100 yd/100 g, 5,000 yd/lb, 10,000 m/kg, laceweight, Claudia Hand Painted Yarns), Passion Fruit, 830 yd. 8/2 Tencel, Deep Coral, 145 yd; Taupe 145 yd; Gray Mauve, 90 yd.

Other Matching sewing thread.

Most of the Southwest Wrap is woven in Tencel (the brand name for lyocell, a regenerated cellulose fiber made from dissolving bleached wood pulp). Tencel shares many characteristics with rayon, particularly its sheen and drape, making it an ideal candidate for a warp-emphasis or warp-faced weave. A skein of handpainted silk with similar characteristics that I chose to use as weft inspired the Tencel color choices in the warp. The fabric is woven with warp stripes, but the garment design places the warp stripes horizontally across the body; a slit in the center of the fabric becomes the neck opening.

WARP MEASUREMENTS

Total warp ends 1,058 (see Warp Color Order).

Warp length 2¾ yd (allows for take-up, shrinkage, and 32" loom waste).

SETTS

EPI 20, 30, and 40 (2/dent, 3/dent, 4/dent in a 10-dent reed; sley the two center dents 5/dent; see the Warp Color Order).

PPI 16.

FABRIC MEASUREMENTS

Width in reed 36⅖".

Width after washing 34".

Woven length (measured under tension on the loom) 65".

Length after washing 61½" in center, 63½" at edges.

Length after sewing 59" in center, 61½" at edges.

Take-up and shrinkage 7% in width, 10% in length.

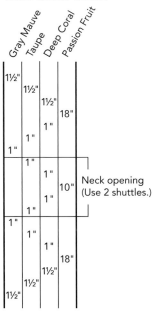

Weft Color Order

Warp Color Order

							8x	8x							
352	30	30	30	30	20	20	2	2	20	20	30	30	30	30	Deep Coral
352	30	30	30	30	20	20	2	2	20	20	30	30	30	30	Taupe
354	30	30	30	30	20	20	2	2*	2	20	20	30	30	30	30	Gray Mauve
1,058	20 epi 2/dent	30 epi 3/dent	40 epi 4/dent	40 epi 4/dent	40 epi 4/dent	30 epi 3/dent	20 epi 2/dent								

*Sley 1 of these center 2 Gray Mauve ends in the same dent as the
4 Coral/Taupe ends to the left and the other in the same dent as the
4 Coral/Taupe ends to the right so that the center 2 dents each have 5 ends.

Washing

Tie loose knots in the warp to secure the waste yarn for washing and also machine zigzag the edges just inside the waste yarn.

Machine wash with a mild detergent on a gentle cycle in warm water with warm rinse for about 20 minutes (note that this amount of agitation works with my front-loading washer; make adjustments for your machine; see Washing, pages 118–119. Lay flat to dry. Trim the waste areas to the machine zigzagging. Steam the fabric using a fabric steamer or an iron (see Steaming vs Pressing, page 120).

Assembly and Sewing

Fold up both raw edges about ⅜". Press gently with an iron. Fold up again about ½" and pin the hem in place. Using an overcast hem stitch (see page 121), sew the hem along the folded edge. Press again gently.

During wear, the warp threads will tend to pull apart at each end of the neck slit. To reinforce these points, with Gray Mauve needleweave a triangle of weft threads in the gap between the warp threads on each side of the slit (see Reinforcing the Neck Slit below). If this area further stretches over time, you can reinforce on the underside with bias tape.

Weaving

Wind a warp of 1,058 ends following the Warp Color Order. Use your preferred method to warp the loom for plain weave, sleying 2/, 3/, 4/, or 5/dent as shown in the Warp Color Order and centering for 36⅖". Tie the warp onto the front apron rod.

Spread the warp by weaving a header using waste yarn. Because there isn't any fringe in this design, you can start weaving the fabric as soon as the warp is spread. Weave plain weave with 1 shuttle following the Weft Color Order. When you reach the section for the neck opening, change to 2 shuttles. Take each shuttle from the selvedge to the center and bring it out of the shed between the 2 center Gray Mauve warp threads. Change the shed and take each shuttle back to the original selvedge and repeat (see Weaving a Slit, page 91). When you finish the slit section, continue, following the Weft Color Order, with 1 shuttle. End with about 1" of plain weave in waste yarn to secure the edge and then remove the fabric from the loom allowing enough warp fringe at each end to tie temporary knots for securing the waste yarn.

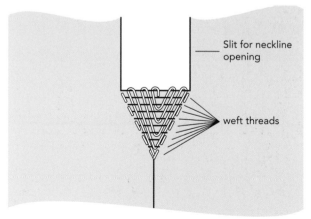

Reinforcing the Neck Slit

CHAPTER 4

Designing

Are you intimidated by the very idea of choosing yarns and colors to weave a fabric for a garment that you also design and sew? If so, it's understandable; most weavers are. Besides, if you find project instructions for something you like, why not just make that? You can, but even then you may need to refine or change the instructions for any number of reasons. The information in this chapter can help you get started, whether your goal is to create original garment designs or to refine a design to suit you and your equipment.

Most handwoven garments fall into one of three categories: loom-shaped, low-sew, or cut-and-sew. Every project in this book is either loom-shaped or low-sew. Because the loom usually yields a rectangular piece of cloth, for centuries rectangular cloth has been transformed into wonderful garb (see page 55)—tunics and huipils (**1**); ponchos, saris, and sarongs (**2**); and kimonos (**3**), as well as hipparis, capes, caftans, shawls,

and more. The Quechquemitl Wrap and the Striped Ruana were influenced by these basic shapes.

Low-sew garments have some minimal shaping, either on the loom or off—a neckline and/or sleeve may be cut from the cloth with little cloth waste. For the low-sew garments in this book, look at the Checkered Sweater, Crème de la Crème Poncho, Sherbet Shrug,

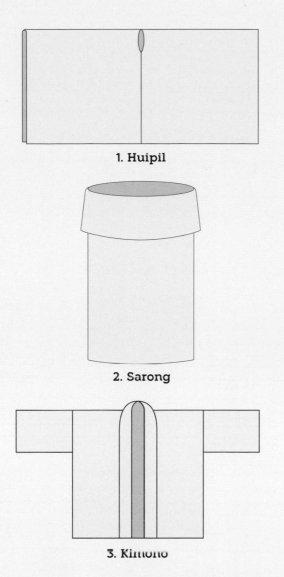

1. Huipil

2. Sarong

3. Kimono

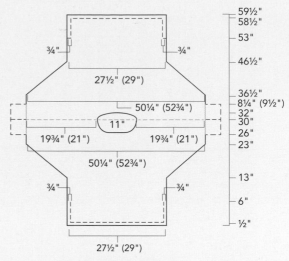

59½"
58½"
53"
46½"
¾"   ¾"
27½" (29")
36½"
8¼" (9½")
50¼" (52¾")
32"
11"
30"
19¾" (21")   19¾" (21")
26"
23"
50¼" (52¾")
13"
¾"   ¾"
6"
½"
27½" (29")

Knitting Schematic

and Wabi Sabi Jacket. Low-sew garments do require planning in order to minimize waste.

Cut-and-sew generally means weaving a cloth and then placing and cutting out multiple pattern pieces beyond a simple neckline or sleeves.

Designing a Garment

Garment shapes can be observed all around you—in the clothing woven by other weavers, displayed in clothing stores, hanging in your own closet in garments that look good on you. Even if a particular garment might not work with handwoven cloth, its general shape might be one you can use.

Get to know your body shape in order to choose styles that look best for your silhouette. Are you top heavy or bottom heavy? Round or hourglass? Understanding your silhouette can inform your decisions about where to add interest or texture as well as choosing a style. Belts enhance a slender waist, but might not be attractive on a thicker one. A long jacket with side pleats will flatter a figure with wider hips.

PATTERNS

If you're a crocheter, knitter, or sewer, you probably have patterns—lots of them. And if you don't, there are many available online to download. Often, a schematic (scaled drawings of knitted or crocheted pattern pieces; see the example above) for a sweater is suitable for a woven garment, such as the one I used for the Checkered Sweater. You can also use commercial sewing patterns or a store-bought garment you'd like to reproduce in handwoven fabric. The following steps apply to all.

There are a few key elements to consider if you are going to choose a pattern created for a different fiber technique than woven cloth. Knit and crochet fabrics drape very differently from the way woven fabrics drape, and the specific yarn and stitches also influence their drape. When I select a crocheted or knitted

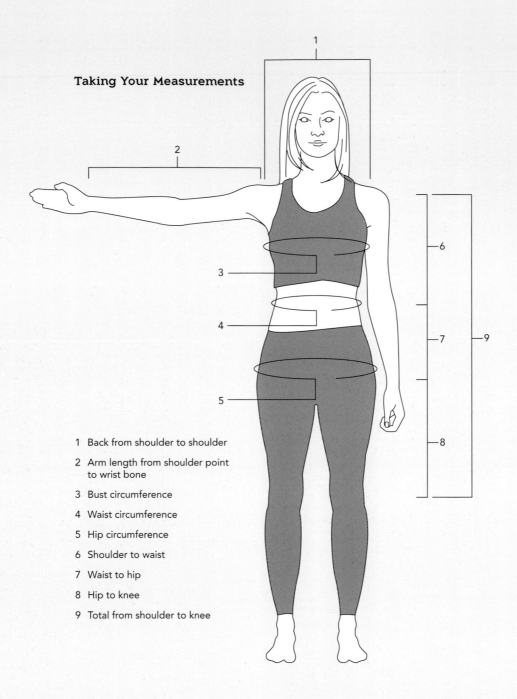

Taking Your Measurements

1 Back from shoulder to shoulder

2 Arm length from shoulder point
to wrist bone

3 Bust circumference

4 Waist circumference

5 Hip circumference

6 Shoulder to waist

7 Waist to hip

8 Hip to knee

9 Total from shoulder to knee

schematic to use as a pattern for a woven one, it's not that I want to re-create the fabric in a woven form— I just like the shape of the garment and think it will work with handwoven cloth. For sewing patterns, find non-form-fitting styles with simple, straight lines. Avoid garments requiring darts. Many simple commercial patterns by Butterick, Kwik Sew, and Vogue, as well as by independent designers, are available.

YOUR MEASUREMENTS

The project garments in this book are not formfitting and most are outerwear or accessories. But even

Choose patterns with simple shapes for handwoven cloth.

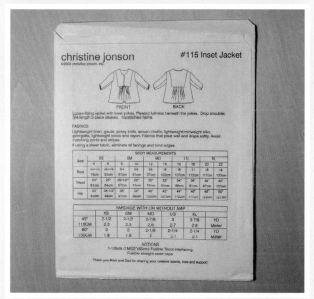

Check your measurements against the pattern measurements.

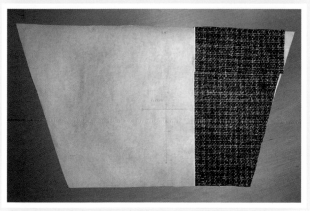

Lines on pattern pieces can aid alignment with woven pattern

with accessories, as in the case of the Ribbon Collar, you need to know your neck measurement and how far you want the collar to drape and to check these measurements against the instructions, adjusting the collar length as needed. So, too, for the Blooming Scarf; the placement of the closure slit should work with your measurements. These are all reasons to make a muslin (a replica of the garment or accessory in scrap fabric of similar weight to the garment you are planning) before you wind the warp.

But what about other adjustments to consider for your shape and height? Take your measurements as shown on page 56 to use for the garments in this book as well as for other garments.

YOUR MEASUREMENTS VS THE PATTERN

The first step is to look at the pattern, schematic, or pattern measurement chart and check your measurements against them, taking ease into consideration. Ease has to do with the garment's purpose, comfort, and fit. For the circumference of an outerwear garment, allow at least 6" of ease, for a vest, about 3", for example. Also think about the pattern choice in terms of the weaving width of your loom. Your loom must accommodate the width of the widest piece, or you'll need to weave it in two pieces; how will the garment look with a seam?

MAKE PATTERN ADJUSTMENTS

Make notations on the pattern where adjustments need to be made (width, length, or changes to shape or size). For knitting schematics, you can photocopy the schematic pieces and mark these. Then, on butcher paper, draw and cut out a full-scale pattern piece for the sleeves, back, front(s), etc. Be sure to add a ½" seam allowance and mark any special notes on each pattern piece. If your handwoven cloth has a distinct woven pattern (striping or checks, for example), you may want to make a line drawing on the pattern pieces so you have a visual example of how these pieces need to line up.

For sewing patterns, open up the package, select the pattern pieces needed, separate each piece, and press the pieces flat. For adjustments to a pattern piece, amend the length of the pattern first before making other alterations. Be sure to keep the grain line straight. Most patterns will delineate "lengthen

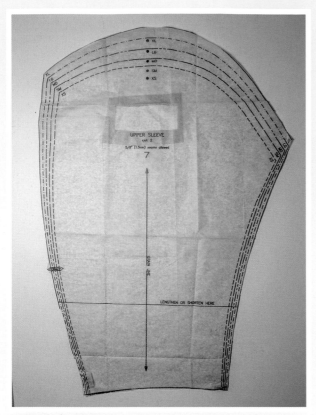

Pattern pieces are often marked "Lengthen or shorten here."

Make a muslin and try it on a dress form, if you have one.

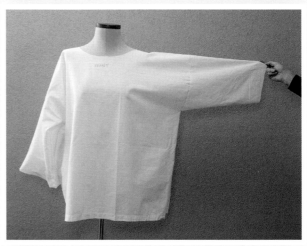

Check length, width, length of sleeve, neck opening, etc.

or shorten here." When you are lengthening a piece, place butcher paper underneath the cut area to fill the gap. Pin the new piece in place to position; tape. When you are shortening a piece, pin in place, check the measurements, and tape. If you are reducing the width of a piece by anything more than 1", make the adjustment in a few places to distribute the resizing evenly.

MAKE A SAMPLE GARMENT

Now you're ready to make a muslin example of the garment that you can try on for fit before making the actual garment out of your handwoven cloth. Place the fabric for your muslin on a large flat surface. Lay out the pattern pieces flat, with no foldlines, the same way they will be placed on the handwoven cloth (on the grainline, running lengthwise or crosswise). Be economical. Go for minimal waste because that is what you will want to do for your handwoven cloth as well. All the information you gain from this step will be important when it comes time to cut your actual cloth.

When you have all the pattern pieces in place, pin them and then cut out each one. Machine straight stitch; there is no need to finish off hems or the neckline. The sewing on this muslin does not have to be tidy or finished the way it will be on your garment. Once the muslin is made, try it on a dress form if you have one your size or put the muslin on and stand in front of a full-length mirror. (You may need a friend's assistance for this.) Check the length and width of the body section. Is there enough ease? Is it short or long enough for your height and shape? What about the sleeve length? Is the neck opening large enough to accommodate an additional edging that may pull the neckline in a bit? Take a marker and make notes directly on the muslin. If the neck opening needs to be larger, mark and cut a new neckline. Pin up the sleeve or bottom hem.

Now what? All changes require making new pattern pieces. If your adjustments are minimal (a shorter/longer sleeve or body length, a bit wider or lower neckline), then you don't have to make a new muslin. But for anything beyond that (a change in shape, a smaller neckline opening), make another muslin and get the fit right before moving to your handwoven cloth.

PLANNING THE LAYOUT

Your loom width must be considered when you lay out the pattern pieces. Cut a piece of the muslin fabric or butcher paper the weaving width of your loom. Lay the piece out flat with no foldlines. Now take your pattern pieces with all their notations as to what has to match pattern-wise—grainline, slit placements, edge treatments, and any other features—and lay them out on the muslin or paper with as little waste as possible. When you have everything just right, take a photo of the layout or sketch it, because you'll need this guide to lay out the pieces on the handwoven cloth. Measure the width and length occupied by the pattern pieces and add for draw-in, take-up, shrinkage, and loom waste. You now know how wide and how long the warp needs to be.

If you want to make one of the garments in this book and your loom isn't wide enough to follow the instructions given, try alternative layouts as described above. A few simple modifications in length can be made to any of the garments. For instance, the Sherbet Shrug's fit is based on the length of the arms and the width of the back. The Shades of Green Vest is easy to lengthen if you want a longer vest, etc.

These samples each use the same warp (horizontal in the photo) with different wefts.

Designing and Weaving the Cloth

The specific yarns—their fiber content, color, grist, twist, and texture—and the weave structure you select will greatly affect the drape of your garment (see Yarn, pages 11–15). When you have chosen both the yarn and the structure suitable for the garment style you are making, the next step is to wind color wraps to determine the sett and also plan the colors and their orders.

CHOOSING YARN COLORS

How particular colors come to be used in a particular garment makes me think of the chicken or the egg—what comes first? Having the yarns you want to use and then designing a garment around them or having the design and then choosing yarns and colors? Let's assume you've followed the steps above and have the garment design and yarns you want to use in mind, and now you want to choose colors.

I often hear people say they're not good at working with color. Color choices are complex in weaving because of the colorplay between warp and weft, as well as among yarns and textures. I can't count the number of times I've wound beautiful warps for mohair throws only to be disappointed when the weft entered the picture. Yet another reason to sample!

Choosing color combinations can be done many ways. One of the simplest is to find a photo you like of a painting or a landscape (I've often used Sierra Club calendars) or of ethnic textiles. Then pull yarns from your stash that come close to matching the printed colors. Check their fiber content to make sure they work together (see Yarn, pages 11–15). Then start blending some visually by twisting them together. Does one color jump out more than another? Are they close in value? Do you want more or less texture? With too much variety, a special yarn can get lost in the mix; in this case, simplify. Use a solid-colored or smooth yarn as the predominant warp and weft threads and highlight the special yarn, as in the Quechquemitl Wrap, the Sherbet Shrug, and the Monet Möbius.

Color wraps—wrapping yarns around a cardboard strip—are the best way to test the combinations. You can mix them one-and-one (for a complete blend) or arrange them in varying proportions of colors or in a specific warp-striping sequence (see Planning Stripes, page 49). I prefer to use white or black cardboard for wraps—white if my colors lean toward dark values, black if they lean toward light values. You can also use gray.

When you are satisfied with your choices, you can use the arrangement to weave a sample and test out wefts (see Sample!, pages 38–39).

WEAVING

Now weave the cloth following your plan and wash, dry, and steam or press the final piece.

Making the Garment

All the steps you've taken so far should make the next steps trouble-free.

CUTTING THE CLOTH

1. Line up the pattern pieces following your layout plan.

2. Pin the pattern to the fabric. Don't cut anything until you have positioned all the pieces.

3. With sharp scissors, cut out each piece. Keep the pattern attached to the piece until you're ready to finish the raw edges.

Ethnic textiles, photos, and artwork can provide color inspiration.

Blend colors (as for warp and weft) by twisting yarns together.

Plan stripe arrangements by making yarn "wraps."

4. Mark the pieces with sewing thread or another visual marker as necessary for matching sleeves and body pieces, buttonholes, and slits.

SEWING

After you've cut out your pattern pieces, you'll probably need to stabilize the raw edges before you do any construction. If so, machine zigzag the edges, then move on to sewing the garment. Project instructions in this book give specific sewing steps for seams and hems. For additional seam treatments, see pages 120–121.

LOOM-SHAPED GARMENTS

Many of the steps mentioned in this chapter are applicable to loom-shaped garments. For the Striped Ruana, for example, make a sample muslin because you'll need to adjust for your height, your width, and the position of the belt openings. Plan the layout after making these adjustments to determine warp width and length. If you're working on a narrower loom, you may need to weave the garment in four panels instead of two. For the Striped Ruana and the Loopy Tabard, no cutting is required. For the Crème de la Crème Poncho, only the neck opening requires any cutting.

DETERMINING THE NECKLINE OPENING

Whether you're cutting the neckline opening or shaping it on the loom, you need to determine how big the opening needs to be, taking into account how much extra space is needed for the finishing treatment (knitted ribbing, attached collar, or other neckline trim) and what type of neckline shape is desired (round, square, or V, for example).

Measure your head circumference and divide by two (for example, a circumference of 22" divided by two equals 11"). Measure straight down from the top shoulderline (where a shoulder seam would be placed) at one side of your neck (A) to where you want the finished neckline to fall at center front (B) and then do the same from the top shoulderline (A) to the neckline at center back (C).

Next, on sturdy paper (several inches wider and longer than your head circumference) make a template: Make a mark in the center (X). Take half of your head circumference (in this example, 11") and, centering that measurement on X parallel to the top and bottom edges of the paper, mark a point at each end of the measurement (A). Mark B the distance from A that you measured from the top shoulder to the front neckline; mark C the distance from X that you measured from the top shoulder to the back neckline. Then, using a

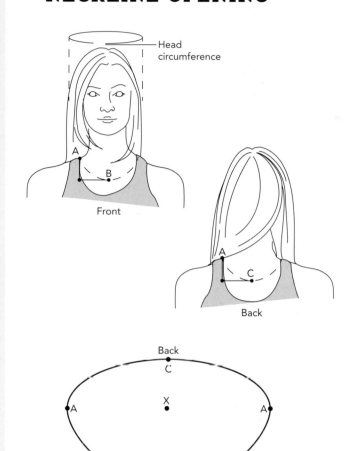

MEASURING FOR THE NECKLINE OPENING

Head circumference

Front

Back

Back
C

X

A

A

B
Front

sewing curve, connect these points (not including X) for a smoothly rounded neckline. For a V-neckline, draw straight lines from A to B and use a curve to shape the back neckline. Make sure your sample muslin includes your neckline shaping.

Quechquemitl Wrap

DESIGN NOTE

The shape of a quechquemitl invites warp stripes, inlay patterning, textured yarns, and other embellishments and trims. It can be woven in almost any yarns, from heavy to lightweight, for all types of weather. A fine merino and soft silk blend are used in this quechquemitl. The wool is worsted-spun, which is smoother and fulls less than woolen spun yarns do, features that are enhanced by the lustrous silk. A handpainted bouclé accent yarn adds color and textural interest, and a crocheted edging provides a defining touch.

EQUIPMENT

2-shaft loom, 4-shaft loom, or rigid-heddle loom, 23" weaving width; 8-dent reed or rigid heddle; 1 shuttle; size G (4.5 m) crochet hook; tapestry needle.

MATERIALS

Warp 8/4 wool/silk (50% wool, 50% silk, 1,120 yd/lb, 2,260 m/kg, Zephyr, JaggerSpun), Steel #006, 405 yd. Rayon bouclé (100% rayon, 325 yd/8 oz skein, 650 yd/lb, 1,312 m/kg, Rayon Loop, Blue Heron Yarns), Dusk, 132 yd.

Weft 8/4 wool/silk, Steel #006, 470 yd.

Other 65 yd Dusk Rayon bouclé for crochet edgings. Sewing thread to match Steel.

The *quechquemitl*, meaning "neck piece" in Nahuatl, is a traditional Mexican woman's upper garment. It is formed of two equal rectangles joined at right angles to make two corners, or points. It can be worn so the points are placed at the center front and center back, or they can be draped from the shoulders, ending at the wrists. The traditional garment is often highly patterned and finished with various types of edgings, from simple to intricate bottom fringing, ribbon around the neckline, and more.

Although the quechquemitl is a simple shape, you'll still want to make a muslin to plan the sizes of the rectangles. The fit over your shoulders and size of the neck opening are important—this will come from the length of the rectangles. The length at the fingertips (or the points) is determined by the width of the rectangles.

WARP MEASUREMENTS

Total warp ends 179 (see Warp Color Order).

Warp length 3 yd (allows for take-up, shrinkage, and 30" loom waste).

SETTS

EPI 8.
PPI 9.

FABRIC MEASUREMENTS

Width in reed 22⅜".

Width after washing 18".

Woven length (measured under tension on the loom) 76".

Length after washing 68".

Take-up and shrinkage 18% in width, 10% in length.

Warp Color Order

	44x		
44		1	Dusk rayon bouclé
135	3	3	Steel wool/silk
179			

Warping and Weaving

Wind a warp of 179 ends following the Warp Color Order. Take care in winding the warp because the yarn is a bit stretchy. If you wind too tightly, the warp will lose length after it is removed from the warping board. Use your preferred method to warp the loom for plain weave.

Spread the warp by weaving a header in plain weave using waste yarn. As soon as the warp is spread, weave 76" of plain weave with Steel wool/silk, maintaining moderate to light tension in order to avoid stretching the yarn (thereby ending up with a shorter piece when the tension is released). End with about 1" in waste yarn to secure the edge and then remove the fabric from the loom.

Washing

Secure the raw edges with machine zigzagging, remove the waste yarn, and trim along zigzagging. Machine wash, warm with a warm rinse, on a gentle cycle using a mild detergent for about 20 minutes (note that this amount of agitation works with my front-loading washer; make adjustments for your machine; see Washing, pages 118–119). Lay flat to dry. Steam using a fabric steamer or an iron (see Steaming vs Pressing, page 120).

Assembly and Sewing

With the fabric still flat, measure to the center of the length of fabric, remove one weft thread, and cut across the warp. Immediately machine zigzag both cut edges to prevent raveling. Follow the instructions on the layout diagram to make the unique quechquemitl shape. Pin the joined edges (make sure the zigzagged edge is on the same side of the garment in both seams; this will be the wrong side). On the right side, with the Steel wool/silk threaded in a tapestry needle, stitch two rows of running stitches along the top of each seam, the first one along the second warp thread from the selvedge and the other one along the fourth warp thread from the selvedge. The running stitches

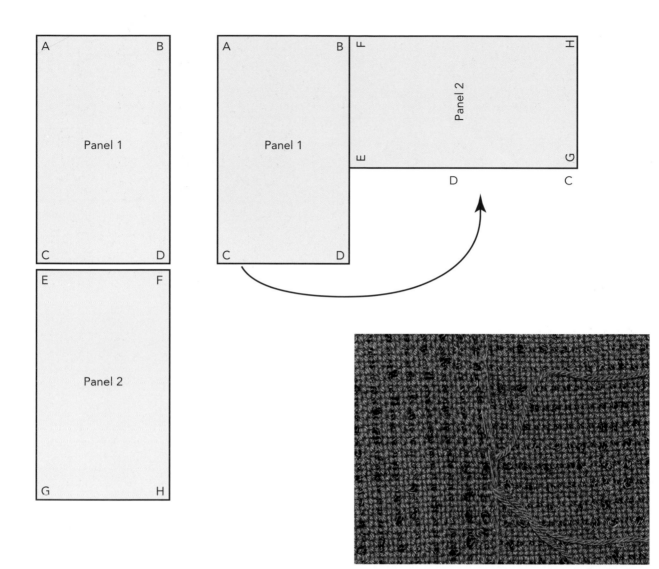

should be short in length, making them almost invisible. On the wrong side and using matching sewing thread, whipstitch the zigzagged seam allowance to secure.

Finishing

Using a size G crochet hook and the Dusk bouclé yarn, work one row of single crochet along the bottom edge of the garment (see Crocheted Edgings, page 122). The crochet stitch should be worked over 2 picks inside the edge and every other pick or warp thread. Single crochet two rows around the neckline in the same way, decreasing slightly on the second row of crocheting to draw the neckline in a bit.

Join the edges with a running stitch using the wool/silk yarn.

Use a size G crochet hook to work a row of single crochet.

Sherbet Shrug

DESIGN NOTES

Usually, a shrug is made of a rectangular piece of fabric. The long part of the rectangle is worn horizontally; the fabric is folded lengthwise and the ends seamed along the selvedges to become sleeves. When a handwoven fabric is used for a shrug, the warp therefore usually runs horizontally across the back and down the arms. Because of this construction, a wider warp means a longer shrug down the back. Read the chapter on Designing to see how to measure your body to determine the right length for you and always make a muslin to check the fit before determining the warp width and length.

In sketching the shrug design, I had first planned a standard shape with a gathered sleeve edge (see Layout 1, page 70) until I looked through a Japanese sewing book and saw a dress with a ruffled sleeve—an idea I immediately adapted! One challenge was how to weave the body (a wide piece) and the sleeve ruffles (two narrow pieces) without excessive fabric waste (compare Layouts 2 and 3).

The beauty of a shrug is that it can be woven from many different fibers and types of yarns to become a casual wrap, a dressy wrap, or anything in between. This version is a light, airy, wisp of a shrug that can add flair—and warmth—to bare shoulders on a cool summer eve, yet it is also elegant enough for a special occasion.

EQUIPMENT

2-shaft loom, 4-shaft loom, or rigid-heddle loom, 24" weaving width; 10-dent reed or rigid heddle; 1 shuttle.

MATERIALS

Warp Kid mohair/nylon blend (70% kid mohair, 30% nylon, 4,450 yd/lb, 8,980 m/kg, Kid Mohair Lace Weight, Louet), Coral #24, 620 yd. Alpaca/silk blend (70% baby alpaca, 30% silk, 460 yd/50 g skein, 4,210 yd/lb, 8,485 m/kg, Silky Alpaca Lace, Classic Elite), 196 yd.

Weft Kid mohair/nylon blend, Coral #24, 660 yd.

Other Matching sewing thread.

WARP MEASUREMENTS

Total warp ends 233 (see Warp Color Order).

Warp length 3½ yd (allows for take-up, shrinkage, and 27" loom waste).

SETTS

EPI 10.
PPI 10.

FABRIC MEASUREMENTS

Width in reed 23⅓".

Width after washing 21".

Woven length (measured under tension on the loom) 99" (3" waste-yarn section, 52" body, 2" waste-yarn section, 40" ruffle section, 2" waste-yarn section).

Length after washing 89" (2½" waste-yarn section, 47" body, 1¾" waste-yarn section, 36" ruffled section, 1¾" waste-yarn section).

Take-up and shrinkage 10% in width and length.

Warp Color Order

	28x				
56	1		1		alpaca/silk
177	7	1		5	2	kid mohair/nylon blend
233					

Weaving

Wind a warp of 233 ends following the Warp Color Order. Use your preferred method to warp the loom (see the Striped Mohair Shawl, page 42, for tips for warping and weaving with mohair). Spread the warp in plain weave using a smooth nonfulling waste yarn for about 3" (see Using Waste Yarn, page 15). For the shrug body: Weave 4 picks with Coral Kid Mohair, beating firmly (almost weft-faced) to create a secure raw edge. Then continue weaving plain weave with Coral but beat lightly at 10 ppi until the fabric measures 52". End the body section with 4 picks of Coral, beating firmly as at the beginning. Weave 2" with waste yarn to separate pieces. For the ruffle: Weave 4 picks, beating firmly, then beat lightly at 10 ppi until fabric measures 40". End the ruffle section with 4 picks, beating firmly. Weave 2" with waste yarn and remove the fabric from the loom, allowing about 4" warp length beyond the last waste-yarn section.

Washing

Tie loose knots in the warp at both raw edges to secure the waste yarn for wet-finishing (this will keep the fringe warp threads from tangling and matting). Machine wash with a mild detergent on a gentle cycle in warm water with a warm rinse for about 20 minutes (note that this amount of agitation works with my front-loading washer; make adjustments for your machine; see Washing, pages 118–119). Lay flat to dry. Remove all waste yarn; steam with a fabric steamer or an iron; see Steaming vs Pressing, page 120.

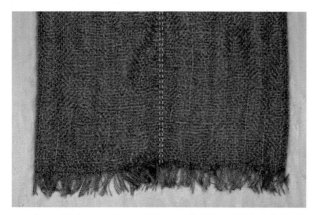

Overlap selvedges and sew two rows of running stitches for 7".

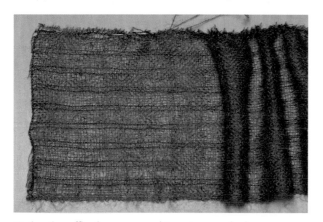

Gather the ruffle along one machine- zigzagged edge.

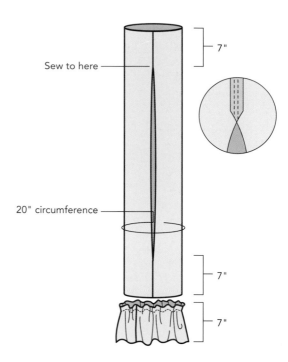

Sew to here

20" circumference

7"

7"

7"

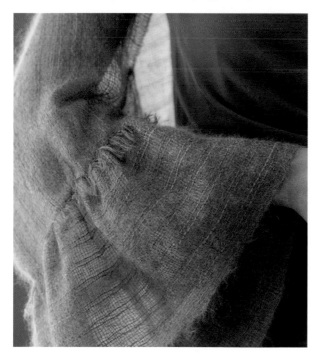

Assembly and Sewing

Trim the warp fringe to about 1" at both ends of the length of fabric. Cut the body and ruffle sections apart in the middle of the 2" area where you removed the waste yarn. Ruffles: Measure 7" from each selvedge to mark the width of each ruffle and remove a few warp threads at these points along the length of the ruffle section to make cutting guides and then cut. Machine zigzag all raw edges of the two ruffles, trim to zigzagging, and set them and the woven section between them aside.

Fold the shrug body to form a tube, overlapping the two selvedges by ½" and pin for 7" from each end. With Coral Kid Mohair, sew two rows of running stitches about ¼" apart along each 7" seam.

FOR EACH RUFFLE

Using matching sewing thread and a handbasting stitch, sew along the 36" raw edge just inside the machine zigzagging and pull the basting stitch to gather until the raw edge measures 20". Machine straight stitch on top of the basting thread to secure the gathering. Bring the short ends of the ruffle together and using matching sewing thread, handsew a seam to join them ½" from the raw edges using a backstitch (see page 121).

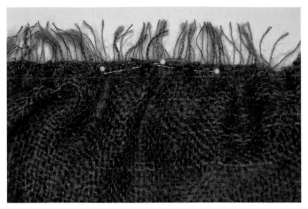

Pin the ruffle into the sleeve opening and sew with a backstitch.

With right sides together, pin the ruffle into the sleeve opening of the shrug body. The ruffle goes under the fringe at the edge of the sleeve opening so the fringe lies on top of the ruffle seam. Sew this seam by hand with a backstitch using Coral yarn.

Use a buttonhole stitch (see page 121) to cover the raw edges of all zigzagged seam allowances.

Finishing

Lightly steam the entire shrug with a fabric steamer or an iron (see Steaming vs Pressing, page 120). Handpress the seams as necessary so they lie flat when the garment is worn.

LAYOUT OPTIONS

Layout 1 is a standard layout for a shrug (without ruffled sleeves). Both Layouts 2 and 3 are for a shrug with ruffled sleeves (the weaving directions and the shrug shown here use Layout 2).

The handpainted alpaca/silk warp threads used in this shrug produce soft stripes that run vertically in the warp but are horizontal in the finished shrug. The stripes in the ruffle run in the opposite direction from the body with Layout 2. With Layout 3, they run in the same direction. The ruffles in Layout 3 use two fabric pieces per ruffle, each cut from the warp width, resulting in two side seams (to join the short ends of the two pieces). The side seams are selvedge edges, so these seam allowances have no raw edges. Instead, the seam allowance

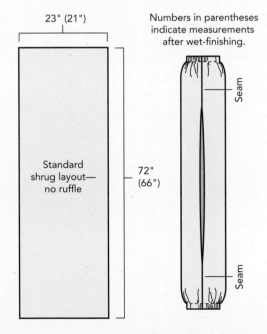

23" (21")

Numbers in parentheses indicate measurements after wet-finishing.

Standard shrug layout— no ruffle

72" (66")

Seam

Seam

Layout 1

where the ruffle is seamed to the body and the hem edges of the ruffles are raw edges and will need to be machine zigzagged or finished in some way. Each ruffle using Layout 3 is about 4" fuller than with Layout 2 (41" circumference instead of 35½").

With Layout 2, the shrug has a selvedge edge at the bottom of the ruffle (no hems necessary), and only one side seam is required (to join the two short ends of the ruffle). A negative with Layout 2 is the fabric that is wasted when the two ruffle pieces are cut from the ruffle section. Mine measured 7" by 36" and became a short neck scarf, so it really wasn't wasted.

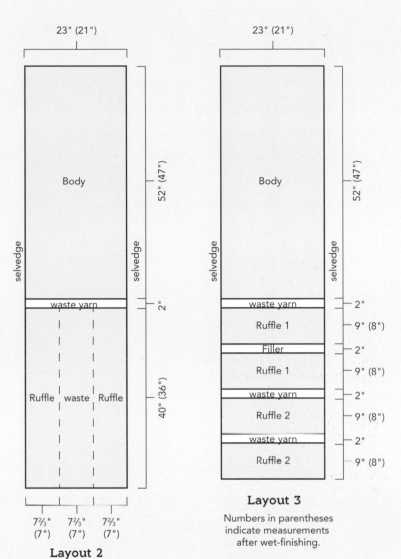

Layout 2

Layout 3

Numbers in parentheses indicate measurements after wet-finishing.

Checkered Sweater

DESIGN NOTES

The color-and-weave draft I selected produces a fabric with an unexpected benefit for a sewer: the woven pattern is the same in both the warp and the weft directions. This means that the pattern pieces can be placed either vertically or horizontally on the fabric, or both. For this sweater, the body pieces are placed vertically, making the side seams the selvedges (therefore needing no finishing treatment for the seam allowances), and the sleeves are placed horizontally, side by side (therefore minimizing fabric waste).

I had originally planned ribbing on the neck, sleeves, and bottom edges, but after sampling, I liked the way the fringe fluffed up, so I decided to use fringe for all the edges instead.

The only fabric waste you'll have from this garment is from the neck opening and the sides of the sleeves—very minimal.

This sweater/poncho was inspired by a photo in a knitting magazine from the 1980s that I had set aside at the time thinking that the sweater's shape would be perfect for a handwoven fabric. Rediscovering it recently, I decided to adapt it for a contemporary garment that would drape and feel like a sweater and be long enough to wear with or without a belt. I first made a muslin based on the sweater's measurements and adjusted for my size.

EQUIPMENT

2-shaft loom, 4-shaft loom, or rigid-heddle loom, 35" weaving width; 6-dent reed or rigid heddle; 2 shuttles.

MATERIALS

Warp Single-ply worsted wool (183 yd/100 g skein, 840 yd/lb, 1,690 m/kg, Donegal Tweed, Tahki) Sage #885, and Tan #801, 420 yd each; Sage is also used for seaming and finishing.

Weft Single-ply worsted wool, Sage and Tan, 380 yd each.

Other Matching sewing thread.

WARP MEASUREMENTS

Total warp ends 210 (see Warp Color Order).

Warp length (measured under tension on the loom) 4 yd (allows for take-up, shrinkage, and 30" loom waste).

SETTS

EPI 6.
PPI 7.

FABRIC MEASUREMENTS

Width in reed 35".

Width after washing 29".

Woven length 110½" (3" waste-yarn section, 68" body, 2" waste-yarn section, 29" sleeves, 2" waste-yarn section, 3½" collar, 3" waste-yarn section; waste is used for fringe).

Length after washing 89¼" (2½" waste-yarn section, 54½" body, 1¾" waste-yarn section, 23½" sleeves, 1¾" waste-yarn section, 2¾" collar, 2½" waste-yarn section).

Take-up and shrinkage 18% in width, 20% in length.

Warp Color Order

	52x		
105	2	1	Tan
105	1	2	Sage
210			

Weaving

Before you start planning this garment, be sure to follow the instructions for measuring and making a muslin (see Making a Sample Garment, pages 58–59). Make any adjustments to weaving width and fabric length before winding the warp. Note that take-up and shrinkage with this singles yarn can be as much as 20%, so determine warp width and length for your desired finished size with that in mind.

Wind a warp of 210 ends following the Warp Color Order. Use your preferred method to warp the loom for plain weave.

Spread the warp by weaving a 3" header using a smooth nonfulling waste yarn (see Using Waste Yarn, page 15). Most of the waste-yarn areas will become the fringed edges of the garment. Using 2 shuttles, weave plain weave, alternating 2 picks of Sage wool with 2 picks of Tan wool, starting the shuttles from opposite sides to carry the inactive wefts up opposite selvedges. Avoid overlapping the beginning and ending of the weft yarns by using the wet-splicing method for a smoother join (see Wet Splicing, page 93).

Weave 68" for the body of the sweater, beginning and ending with Sage. Weave 2" with waste yarn. Weave 29" for the sleeves following the same color order as for the warp, beginning and ending with Sage. Finish with 2" of waste yarn. Weave 3½" for the collar following the same color order, beginning and ending with Sage. End with 3" of waste yarn and then remove the fabric from the loom, leaving 3–4" of warp fringe at each end to tie in temporary knots.

Washing

Tie loose knots in groups of 10–15 warp threads each to secure the last picks of waste yarn at both ends of the fabric. Then remove 2" of the waste yarn immediately next to the first and last Sage weft threads at both ends of the warp, leaving the very last inch of waste weft next to the knots in place at both ends. (The fringe will full but will be kept from overfulling and matting by leaving this waste yarn in place.) Remove all waste yarn between the body section and the sleeves and the body section and the collar.

Remove 14 warp threads down the center of the sleeve section (between the two waste yarn weft areas; see the Layout). The weft yarns in this open section will full to become the fringe on the bottom of each sleeve.

Machine wash the entire length of fabric with a mild detergent on a gentle cycle in warm water with a warm rinse for about 20 minutes (note that this amount of agitation works with my front-loading washer; make adjustments for your machine; see Washing, pages 118–119). Lay flat to dry. Trim the extra knotted warp threads away, remove the remaining waste yarn,

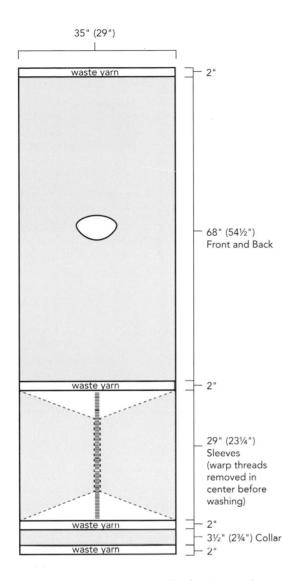

35" (29")

waste yarn — 2"

68" (54½")
Front and Back

waste yarn — 2"

29" (23¼")
Sleeves
(warp threads
removed in
center before
washing)

waste yarn — 2"
3½" (2¾") Collar
waste yarn — 2"

Numbers in parentheses
indicate measurements
after wet-finishing.

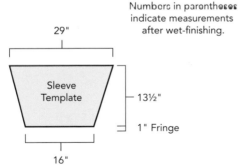

29"

Sleeve
Template

13½"

1" Fringe

16"

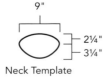

9"

2¼"
3¼"

Neck Template

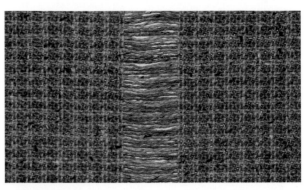

Remove 14 warp threads in the center of the sleeve section.

Place the sleeve template with the wrist end on the fringe.

and steam the fabric and fringe with a fabric steamer or an iron (see Steaming vs Pressing, page 120).

When the fabric is dry, separate the sleeve section from the body and collar sections, cutting along the raw edge of the sleeve section (all the fringe stays with the body and collar sections). Cut the two sleeves apart down the center of the weft-fringe area.

Assembly and Sewing
SLEEVES

Make a full-scale sleeve template. Place the template on each of the sleeve pieces with the top of the sleeve pattern along the selvedge edge (the wrist end of the sleeve will be the weft fringe) and cut out the sleeve (you'll be cutting only the sleeve sides). Machine zigzag the raw edges on the sides of the sleeves. On the back side of the bottom of each sleeve, using a sewing needle and matching thread, sew a running stitch, catching the first row of weft and a warp thread in each stitch to help secure the raw edge. Fluff up the fringe area at the bottom of each sleeve using a brush, brushing from the fringe toward the sleeve body. Set sleeves aside.

THE NECKLINE AND COLLAR

THE SLEEVES

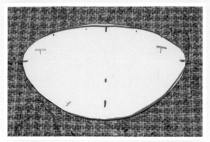

Place, pin, and handbaste around template.

Follow the stitching to cut the opening.

Pin each sleeve to the body section.

Pin the collar to the neck opening, allowing for ease.

Backstitch or crochet collar to neck opening.

Sew together with an invisible joining stitch.

COLLAR

Machine zigzag one raw edge of the collar section and trim off the fringe (the collar will have fringe on one long side only). Align both selvedge ends of the collar (to make a circle) and join them using an invisible joining stitch (see page 120).

MAKING THE NECKLINE OPENING

Make a full-scale template for the neck opening (see Determining the Neckline Opening, page 61). Place the template in the center of the body section (see photos above), marking the neck center and the top shoulder line and pin in place. Using a contrasting thread and long basting stitches, stitch along the outline of the template. Remove the template. Cut out the neck along the inside edge of the basted sewing line. Machine zigzag around the raw edges of the opening.

BODY AND SLEEVES

Lay the body section on a flat surface. Using pins or thread, mark the top shoulder line at each selvedge. On the sleeve pieces, mark the center of the top of each sleeve. With right sides together, pin the sleeve to the body, first to join the sleeve center mark with the top shoulderline mark, then continuing down each side of the body, aligning the woven pattern. Sew the pieces together using an invisible joining stitch with Sage wool threaded in a tapestry needle.

Then, right sides together, pin the body and underarm side seams, aligning the woven pattern. Sew the side seams with an invisible joining stitch using Sage wool and sew the matching zigzagged raw edges of the sleeve seams with a backstitch using Sage wool, again aligning the woven pattern and easing in the fabric as necessary.

ATTACHING THE COLLAR

With right sides together, place the collar around the neck opening, aligning and first pinning the collar seam at the center back neck and then easing the fabric as you pin the rest of the collar to the neck opening. Backstitch or single crochet this seam. (An option is to use single crochet for all of the seams in this sweater as I did; single crochet hides raw edges nicely; see Joining Fabrics Using Single Crochet, page 122).

RIBBED EDGINGS

Pick up stitches to work a k2, p2 ribbing.

Bind off leaving a long end for sewing.

Fold ribbing in half to cover raw edges.

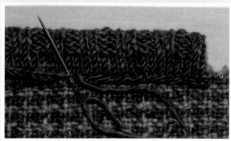

Sew ribbing to fabric edge with a running stitch.

Trim all fringes to the desired length and lightly brush the fringe to fluff. Steam the whole garment with a fabric steamer or an iron (see Steaming vs Pressing, page 120); if the seams pucker, you may need to press them.

Alternate Edgings: Knitted Ribbing

A knitted ribbing provides a clean edging to almost any sweater-like handwoven garment, plus it covers the raw edges of a cut fabric. Follow these steps to use ribbing for the cuffs, bottom, and neckline edge of this woven sweater.

RIBBED COLLAR

Using a size F crochet hook or the tip of a 24" size 8 (5mm) circular needle, pick up 76 stitches under the zigzagged edge of the fabric, about every other warp thread. Because the ribbing will be a k2, p2 rib, the number of picked-up stitches must be divisible by 4. Work in a k2, p2 ribbing for 3" or the desired length, then work ¾" in stockinette stitch. Bind off leaving a long end for sewing. Fold the ribbing in half, using the stockinette-stitch part to cover the raw edges; pin the ribbing in place. Using a running stitch, catch the stitch at the base of the neckline and one from the ribbing edge, and sew around the base of the ribbing.

RIBBED BOTTOM EDGE AND SLEEVE EDGES

Follow the same steps to add a knitted ribbing at the bottom edge of the sweater (use a circular knitting needle) and to the sleeve edges (use double-pointed knitting needles).

Shades of Green Vest

DESIGN NOTES

The vest can be worn open with the scarf hanging freely down the sides, or the edges of the scarf can be overlapped and secured with a special pin to close the vest. You can also vary this design by planning a longer scarf with ends that extend below the vest bottom. Or, the scarf can be attached only to the back neckline of the vest, allowing both ends to be free for wrapping around your neck. If you make a muslin, you can test out a number of design options before planning your warp.

When you first see this vest, you might think the scarf is a separate piece and that the scarf and vest have been woven on different warps. But they are both woven on the same warp using a mohair blend for weft, and the scarf is attached to the vest along the fronts and the back of the neck. Textural interest is created in the scarf by using the mohair blend at two very different densities in the weft, and a handpainted chenille accent yarn adds sparks of color to the vest fabric.

EQUIPMENT

2-shaft loom, 4-shaft loom, or rigid-heddle loom, 12" weaving width; 8-dent reed or rigid heddle; 2 shuttles; tapestry needle.

MATERIALS

Warp 2-ply wool (1,800 yd/lb, 3,630 m/kg, Harrisville Shetland, Harrisville Designs), Ebony #85, 450 yd. Rayon chenille (1,000 yd/lb, 2,018 m/kg), handpainted in variegated golds and pale greens, 60 yd. (This yarn is no longer available. Substitute a handpainted or space-dyed yarn or other novelty yarn in a nonshrinking, nonfulling fiber at about 1,000 yd/lb; undyed rayon chenille at 1,000 yd/lb is available from Henry's Attic.)

Weft for vest Kid mohair/nylon blend (70% kid mohair, 30% nylon; 4,450 yd/lb, 8,980 m/kg, Kid Mohair Lace Weight, Louet), Dark Olive #41, 150 yd. 100% wool (131 yd/100 g, Jackson, Tahki) Moss #007, 150 yd. 2-ply wool (Harrisville Shetland), Ebony, 40 yd.

Weft for scarf Kid mohair/nylon blend, Dark Olive #41, 200 yd.

Other Sewing thread to match the Ebony wool.

WARP MEASUREMENTS

Total warp ends 93 (see Warp Color Order).

Warp length 5¼ yd (allows take-up, shrinkage, and 27" loom waste).

SETTS

EPI 8.
PPI 11.

FABRIC MEASUREMENTS

Width in reed 11⅝".

Width after washing 8" each for the two vest front pieces, 10½" each for the two vest back pieces, and 8" for the scarf.

Woven length (measured under tension on the loom) 160" (2" waste-yarn section, 24" back, 1" waste-yarn section, 24" back, 1" waste-yarn section, 24" front, 1" waste-yarn section, 24" front, 2" waste-yarn section, 56" scarf, 2" waste-yarn section).

Length after washing 147½" (1¾" waste-yarn section, 21" back, ¾" waste-yarn section, 21" back, ¾" waste-yarn section, 21" front, ¾" waste-yarn section, 21" front, 1¾" waste-yarn section, 48" scarf, 1¾" waste-yarn section).

Vest length after washing 20" from shoulder seam to hemmed bottom edge (part of the hem is the trimmed fringe turned under).

Take-up and shrinkage 13% in length, 10% in width.

Weaving

Wind a warp of 93 ends following the Warp Color Order. Use your preferred method to warp the loom for plain weave. Note that the side of the warp with 4 threads of Ebony wool will become the center back.

For the vest, you will be weaving with 2 shuttles; you can carry the Dark Olive Kid Mohair yarn up the selvedge, always on the same side—these floats will be hidden when the invisible joining seam is sewn. Each time you weave 7 picks with the Moss wool, however, begin and end the weft.

Measure carefully as you weave so that each sequence of 11 picks is exactly the same height (1") with the Dark Olive Kid Mohair weft stripe always the same size (⅛") and the Moss wool weft stripe always the same size (⅞") so that when the vest pieces are sewn together, the stripes line up. Keep track of the number of stripe repeats in each vest piece to make sure that you have the same number in each.

Weft Color Order

Warp Color Order

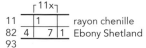

11		1		rayon chenille
82	4	7	1	Ebony Shetland
93				

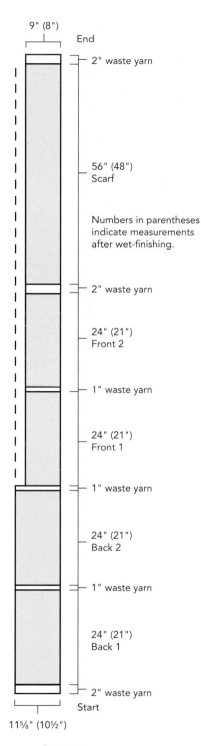

Layout

9" (8")
End
2" waste yarn

56" (48")
Scarf

Numbers in parentheses
indicate measurements
after wet-finishing.

2" waste yarn

24" (21")
Front 2

1" waste yarn

24" (21")
Front 1

1" waste yarn

24" (21")
Back 2

1" waste yarn

24" (21")
Back 1

2" waste yarn
Start

11⅝" (10½")

Spread the warp using a smooth nonfulling waste yarn (see Using Waste Yarn, page 15) for about 2". Begin the first vest back piece by weaving plain weave with Ebony wool for 1½", beating firmly (this will be the hem section). End the Ebony yarn. Then weave the body of the first back piece following the Weft Color Order. When you weave the 4 picks of Dark Olive Kid Mohair, beat firmly, so that they are weft-faced and about ⅛" in height.

End with 1" of Ebony wool for the shoulder seam. Weave 1" using waste yarn. Weave the second vest back piece the same way as the first, ending with 1" using waste yarn.

Now cut 21 warp threads from the side of the warp that has the 4 Ebony wool ends (including these 4 ends), remove them from the reed and heddles, and leave them hanging from the back beam. This will be warp waste, but you can use some of the Ebony strands later for handsewing the seams. The warp is now 9" wide. Follow the same steps for both vest front pieces as for the back pieces, including the 1" sections of waste yarn, but at the end of the second vest front weave 2" with waste yarn (this will become fringe for the scarf).

For the scarf, using only Dark Olive Kid Mohair, weave 4 picks beating very firmly (⅛") and then 7 picks of open plain weave (7 picks = ⅞") and alternate these two densities for 55⅞". End with 4 picks beaten very firmly. Weave 2" with waste yarn and then remove the fabric from the loom leaving 3–4" warp length beyond the last picks of waste yarn to use for tying temporary knots.

Washing

Tie loose knots in the warp to secure the waste yarn at both ends of the fabric. All waste yarn remains in place during the washing process to keep the warp fringe from getting tangled and matted. Machine wash with a mild detergent on a gentle cycle in warm water with warm rinse for about 20 minutes (note that this amount of agitation works with my front-loading washer; make adjustments for your machine; see Washing, pages 118–119). Lay flat to dry. Remove the waste yarn and then steam with a fabric steamer or an iron (see Steaming vs Pressing, page 120).

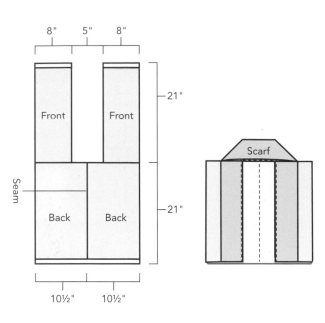

Sewing Layout

Assembly and Sewing
(see Sewing Layout)

Cut pieces apart by cutting through the centers of the waste-yarn sections. Machine zigzag the ends of the vest pieces (not the scarf). Trim the fringe along the zigzagging to ¼".

BACK SEAM

For the center back seam, lay the two back pieces flat, side by side with the two 4-end Ebony wool stripes abutting. Line up the weft stripes and pin the back pieces together along the selvedges. You may need to ease the fabric to align the weft stripes. Using Dark Olive Kid Mohair and a tapestry needle, sew an invisible joining seam by catching wefts, mohair to mohair and wool to wool, including the edge warp thread of each piece in each stitch.

SHOULDER SEAMS

With right sides together, backstitch between the 2nd and 3rd row of Ebony weft closest to the raw edge, leaving a narrow seam allowance on each shoulder.

BACK NECK SEAM

Turn the Ebony section of weaving along the back neck under twice to create a neck facing and stitch as for a hem.

SIDE SEAMS

Align the selvedges of the side seams and sew the seams using Dark Olive Kid Mohair with an invisible joining stitch for 10", starting at the bottom edge on each side. Catch the wefts, mohair to mohair and wool to wool, including the edge warp thread of each piece in each stitch.

BOTTOM HEM

Make a folded hem turning up the ¼" of trimmed fringe and zigzagging and then turning again, leaving about ½" of Ebony showing at the bottom right edge to create a visual border to the vest. Backstitch the hem in place.

SCARF

Steam the scarf. Lightly brush the weft at the fringe ends toward the scarf body to secure; the mohair will form a self-edge. Trim the fringe to 1¼". To attach the scarf to the vest, mark the center of the scarf and, with right sides together, pin to the center back seam. Pin

the scarf ends to the bottom edge of the vest fronts and then continue to pin the scarf to the front edges from the center neck to the bottom, easing the scarf fabric into place around the back neck. Use an invisible joining seam to attach the scarf to the vest body.

Once everything is stitched, steam the final piece with a fabric steamer or an iron (Steaming vs Pressing, page 120).

ALTERNATE LAYOUT

This vest can be woven using a different layout if your loom width is at least 23¼". Weave the back first, then the two front pieces side by side and the two scarf sections side by side with 2 shuttles. The two scarf lengths will have to be seamed together at the center back.

Wind a 3 yd warp of 186 ends following the repeat in the Warp Color Order 23 times, but beginning with 1 Ebony wool end instead of 4. Spread the warp using waste yarn for about 2". Begin the vest back piece by weaving plain weave with Ebony wool for 1½", beating firmly (this will be the hem section). End the Ebony yarn. Then weave the body of the back piece following the Weft Color Order. Cut the center 40 warp threads about 3" beyond the fell and tie in temporary knots at the fell. Pull the cut warp threads out of the heddles and suspend them from the back beam. Now weave the two front pieces side by side with 2 shuttles, 1 for each piece, following the Weft Color Order. Change to Ebony wool and weave plain weave for 1½", beating firmly. Weave 2" with waste yarn (this will become the fringe for the scarf).

For the scarf: With only Dark Olive Kid Mohair as weft, using 2 shuttles, weave 4 picks beating very firmly (⅛") and then weave 7 picks of open plain weave (7 picks = ⅞"); alternate these two densities for 28". End with 4 picks, beating very firmly. Weave 2" with waste yarn and remove the fabric from the loom, leaving 3–4" warp length beyond the last picks of waste yarn.

WASHING, ASSEMBLY, AND SEWING

Tie loose knots in the warp to secure the waste yarn at both ends of the fabric and follow the same washing, finishing, and assembly directions as for the first layout, omitting the center back and shoulder seams. At the back neck, you'll need to needleweave each 3" warp end along the path of the adjacent warp end at the center back for about 1" and trim. Machine zigzag and trim off the fringe on one raw edge of each scarf piece and seam these ends together with a backstitch before attaching the scarf to the vest body (attach the scarf to the body so that when the scarf is folded at the neck, the seam allowance at the center back is on the inside).

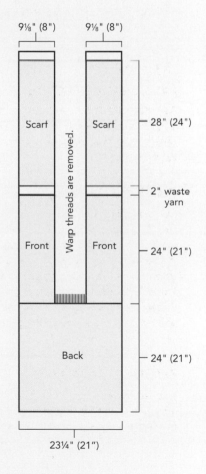

Nancy Waight Paap

I'm a self-taught weaver. Having learned to weave on a loom that was already warped, I got to enjoy the fun and creative aspects of the art first!

My first weaving was a very complicated rug that my mother still owns. I wove a few rugs to master weft-faced weaving and then moved on to very fine silk blouses. What a challenging, quick learning curve! Because I still loved weaving rugs, I would buy enough yarn for one rug, sell it to a store, and buy twice as much yarn to weave two rugs, and so on. I began dyeing my own yarns using the vegetation in northern New Mexico. To make ends meet, I restored Navajo rugs. That, too, was a wonderful learning curve in dyeing and texture.

My love of color and texture increased over the years and is the focus of my current work. I no longer weave rugs, only clothing, using rayon and cotton chenille with its luscious feel, texture, and vibrant colors. Color

I am not afraid to put the strangest of colors together to create new palettes— and texture, always texture for a sense of adventure and movement.

is all around—in nature, cars, fashion, food, magazines, movies, and even my dreams. I am not afraid to put the strangest of colors together to create new palettes—and texture, always texture for a sense of adventure and movement.

Very early in my weaving career I had access to lovely Samoyed undercoat brushings. It was free! I learned to spin and weave it. Today, I have a line of dog-fur coats, hats, jackets, and vests—wonderful fur garments without killing an animal.

Now, I only exhibit my work once a year in a public show so I can get feedback on my designs. Otherwise, I sell in various galleries across the country. I create new styles on the groundwork of previous styles, making a slight change here, a cut there . . . until a new style emerges. Completely new styles go through several "closet" pieces before I'm satisfied. I don't skimp on materials. Considering the time involved, their cost is the least investment you make, and the right materials make all the difference in the finished product.

Presently, I'm intrigued by felting, and I'm learning to combine my weaving scraps into the felt. It's exciting and challenging—another learning curve! It's new to me, and that's what matters.

NANCY WAIGHT PAAP was born in the West Indies. She spent her early childhood in Taos, New Mexico. After living in both England and South Africa, she returned to the Southwest and settled in Santa Fe, New Mexico, in 1968. Nancy was one of the cofounders of the legendary Santa Fe Weaving Gallery and now sells her unique garments through galleries.

Layna Bentley

My fondness for sketching fashion figures at ten years of age led to my pursuit of working and teaching in the field of fashion. My first garments were woven with fat textural yarns at eight ends per inch in simple loose constructions. Through workshops with Virginia West and Margaret Roach Wheeler, I gained insight into choosing appropriate yarn weights and setts for more finely woven clothing.

My first tailored garment design used a 32-inch warp width, leaving so much waste that I shifted to 15- to 20-inch warp widths. Narrow weaving gives me the ability to design as I go. I like the serendipity this provides without being held to a long-range plan, changing direction of color or pattern as I weave. Once the yardage is off the loom and finished, the garment design may take yet another direction.

My garments are all one-of-a-kind classic styles designed to enhance a woman's figure with special details such as piping, embellishments, yoke treatment, and special buttons or closures. Because I sell my work, I'm conscious of different body types. Most women seem to be wider in the hips, so my longer garments have a 4- to 6-inch slit on the side seam to give more room. I may add a tab for reinforcement and decoration.

Because of my narrow warps, the garments must be pieced in the center back, providing an automatic spot for detail. In Brave New Red, I used a twisted rope of the weft yarn tacked to the back seam with a wooden embellishment (photo at lower left, page 87). This keeps the detail on a vertical line and adds no bulk or attention to the wearer's lower half.

I think a garment should be interesting both "coming and going," so my garments typically have an interesting design on the back as well as the front.

I weave plain weave on the same warp as the garment for piping to use as trim. I also like the look of fine soutache and may use more than one row in the ditch of the collar and center front panel (at lower right page 87). Handwoven fabric tends to be bulkier than commercial fabric, even in fine threads, so I use lining fabric for the undercollar to minimize bulk.

I have always been a recycler of scraps, making handbags, notecards and other small items from them. I keep any large pieces or "bad" scarves that have potential for a new life. A favorite design technique is to use large scrap pieces as inspiration for a new garment. I weave new cloth that can be coordinated with the scrap in the same garment, using comparable yarns (weight and fiber).

I think a garment should be interesting both "coming and going," so my garments typically have an interesting design on the back as well as the front.

PHOTOS BY LUANN SMITH

LAYNA BENTLEY has received several awards at the Midwest Weavers Conference as well as being featured artist in 2007. In 2010, she was a featured artist/teacher at the Hillestad Gallery Designer Showcase in Nebraska. She is a frequent fashion show juror and has taught at regional conferences and Convergence.

Joyce Wilkerson

There is magic in creating cloth. Over the years I've developed a way of working that takes me through a number of steps. I keep an ongoing journal of things that attract my eye: photographs I've taken, magazine clippings with great color combinations, interesting architecture, patterns of all sorts, garment shapes, anything intriguing.

Every year I design a collection of fabrics that will become clothing, so I start by thinking about five to eight colorways and how they will look as a group. Reviewing my journal of inspirations is a great way to jumpstart a design project. Then I begin gathering yarns of various weights, colors, and textures.

The warp is the foundation of the cloth, and I color it richly. Because it often gets covered by the weft, I want what does show through to be lively. A range of middle values works well for me, and usually the warp is made up of blended stripes so that darks and lights move across the fabric. Because of production considerations, a single common warp for the entire collection is the best approach for me. Early in my career I learned this the hard way when I received orders for designs from different warps—all with the same deadline. Now, I strive for multiple fabric designs on one warp with one threading.

My background in printmaking has given me a strong interest in graphic designs, and using a 24-shaft computerized dobby loom makes it possible to create complex patterns. The weave structures I use are unit weaves, such as summer and winter and double two-tie. I put on long, narrow sample warps. This design phase allows me to try all sorts of combinations

> Reviewing my journal of inspirations is a great way to jumpstart a design project.

and make plenty of "mistakes." I cut off frequently and wash the fabric to see how it comes together.

The whole process is a dance between the loom and the computer. First I draw patterns and then apply weave structures using WeavePoint software. As I try them out on the loom, it quickly becomes clear what is working and what isn't, and I go back to the computer to make changes. My designs evolve through many permutations. In each fabric I pay close attention to the amount of contrast (dark and light values) in the yarns. This is where the artist's eye decides just how subtle or dynamic the cloth will be.

After graduating from Massachusetts College of Art with a degree in printmaking, **JOYCE WILKERSON** moved to New Mexico and set up her first studio making photo silkscreen prints. In 1974, with the gift of a loom from her loom-maker husband, she became a weaver. An interest in complex-weaves and graphic patterning led her to computerized dobby looms. She has exhibited widely and produces a collection of jackets and vests that sell in galleries around the country.

CHAPTER 5

Weaving Tips and Techniques

With every project you weave, you probably learn something new (unless you weave the same item over and over again). Even though I often use the same fibers and weave structure for my pieces, any change in color combination, garment shape, and/or finishing techniques provides at least one new takeaway.

I taught weaving for years and loved it. Why? Because I had to stay on my toes and learn constantly. I never knew what question a student would ask. Many times the answer could only come from testing out an idea or trying different ways to tackle the same problem. My favorite learning comes from observing skilled weavers, seeing their hand movements, how they use a shuttle, how they wind a warp. I've been awestruck by a Lao weaver tying a knot in a broken silk warp thread—silk sett at 60 or 70 ends per inch—in about a nanosecond. And by a Peruvian weaver handpicking an incredibly intricate warp-faced pattern using a simple wooden stick. While our spoken language wasn't in common, our weaving language was, and I clearly had lots to learn.

Here are some tips I've learned from teachers, fellow students, global artisans, books and videos, or simply trial and error.

LASHING METHOD FOR TYING ON

Instead of tying onto the front apron rod, tie groups of warp threads (about 1–1½" of warp width in each group) in an overhand knot close to the ends of the warp. Position the knot in the same place in each group. Next, using a strong twine five times as long as the weaving width of the cloth, tie one end of the

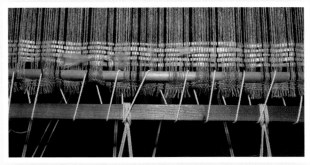

Instead of retying after a sample, lash a stick to the apron rod. (With the lashing method of tying on, the twine passes through the warp groups instead of around the dowel.)

twine onto the apron rod just beyond the warp width on one side. Take the twine through the first knotted group of threads, just above the knot, around the apron rod, into the next knotted group, and continue across the warp, pulling the cord to eliminate the slack in it and in the warp groups. When all warp groups have been caught, temporarily tie the twine onto the apron rod just beyond the last warp group. Tighten the tension on the warp. Even out the tension by moving the cord to remove any slack and patting the warp groups. When the tension is even, make that last knot in the cord permanent and then increase the tension on the warp as needed for weaving.

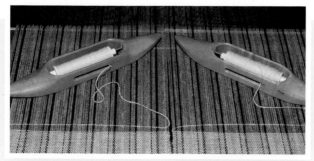

Use two shuttles to weave a vertical slit in the cloth.

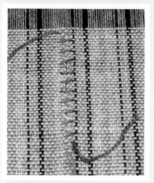

Sew the slit closed temporarily to prevent distortion.

Add a "selvedge" thread on each side to reinforce the slit.

Weave in thread markers for accurate measurements.

RETYING AFTER SAMPLING

I can be pretty certain about a warp's color order (from making a wrap) and sett (from knowing the yarn), but not always about the effect of weft yarn and color. You can't make a final weft choice when the sample is still on the loom because you need to wash it, handle it, and view it from a distance. To cut off a sample and tie the warp back on for more sampling, here's a method that saves both warp and time: After weaving the first sample, weave 1–1½" of very firm plain weave using a nonslippery yarn. Next, make a plain-weave shed and insert a smooth stick longer than the warp is wide and about as thick as your apron rod. Then weave another inch of loose plain weave

in waste yarn. Cut off the sample, leaving the 1–1½" of plain weave, the stick, and the loose waste-yarn section hanging from the reed. Now lash the woven-in stick to the apron rod (see the photo, page 90), tighten the tension, and you're ready to weave again.

WEAVING A SLIT

You can weave a vertical slit in a cloth by using two shuttles for each weft row, one shuttle on each side of the slit. Mark where the slit is to be made with a thread. Make a shed and weave with one shuttle from one selvedge to this marker and weave with the other shuttle to the marker from the other selvedge, bringing both shuttles out of the cloth at the marker. Change sheds and weave each shuttle back to its respective selvedge. Repeat these steps until the slit is the desired length, being careful not to draw in along the slit. End the use of one shuttle and resume weaving with the other shuttle from selvedge to selvedge. If the slit area tends to pull open, sew it closed with a temporary seam using a nonfulling yarn. This thread will be removed after finishing.

If the slit is in an area that will receive repeated stress or abrasion, you can add an extra "selvedge" thread at each side of the slit.

MEASURING

Use thread markers along the selvedge to mark every 10" or so (choose your measurement and be consistent) while the cloth is under tension. (Don't unroll the fabric from the cloth beam to measure it.) Place a lightweight, nonfulling yarn into the open shed along with the weft for about 2" in from the selvedge. If you are matching pattern pieces and want to identify specific seams or positions to match, use different-colored threads to denote them and write down what they mean. Remove any markers after assembly and sewing.

USING MULTIPLE WEFTS

When you are using more than one weft, carry the inactive wefts up the selvedges instead of cutting and ending them. In cases where this might cause unwanted floats along the selvedge for more than ½", take the active shuttle around them for a smooth edge. If the selvedges will be hidden inside a seam or get covered by an edging, you can carry yarns a few inches without needing to enclose them.

MAKING A YARN BUTTERFLY

Hold your open hand palm up. Place a 4–6" tail of the yarn on your palm between your little finger and ring finger and bring the rest of the yarn around the back of your hand and to the front between your thumb and index finger. Then, in a figure-eight path, wind so the yarn goes around the little finger and thumb, building up on the palm of your hand. Make ten wraps or so and then cut the yarn, leaving about a 6" tail. Take the original tail of yarn and wrap it round the crossed threads at the center and make several half hitches. The butterfly will release yarn when the ending tail is pulled.

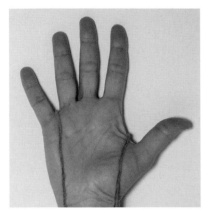 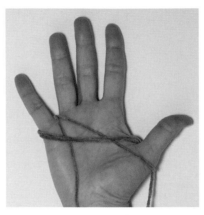 

For a butterfly, place the yarn on your hand.　　*Wind the yarn following a figure-eight path.*　　*Leave a tail and wrap it around the center.*

WEAVING WITH RIBBON

To wind a stick shuttle with ribbon yarn that comes in a skein, place the skein on a skein winder and then wind the yarn directly onto the shuttle, keeping the ribbon flat and not stretching it as you wind. If the ribbon twists as it comes off the winder, you can easily untwist it.

To end a ribbon weft and start a new one, taper the ends of both for about 1½". Overlap the ends in the shed by 1–1½" and beat in place.

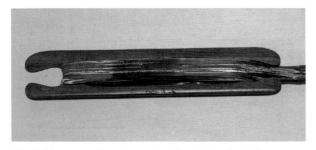 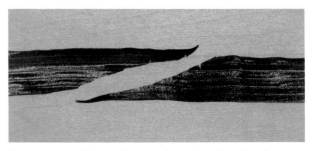

Wind ribbon yarn directly onto the shuttle, keeping it flat.　　*To start a new ribbon weft, taper the ends and overlap them.*

WET SPLICING

Wet splicing joins the ends of two wool yarns, usually singles. Moisten your palms. Take the end of one yarn and the end of the other in your palm from opposite directions and overlap them for about 2". Briskly rub your palms together until you no longer see the ends.

DRY SPLICING

Dry splicing joins the ends of two plied yarns. Untwist the plies at the end of each yarn and pull off about 1½" of one of the plies in each. Overlap the ends in the shed. Beat. After washing and finishing, the joining becomes invisible.

To wet splice: overlap the ends in your moistened palm.

Untwist the plies of the new and old wefts.

Briskly rub both palms together until the ends are joined.

Remove about 1½" of one ply on each and overlap the ends.

MAINTAINING AN EVEN FELL

Always grab the beater in the center to beat, alternating hands with each pick. Otherwise, the fell of the cloth can become slanted toward the side of the hand you used. For the fabrics in this book, only one beat should be needed to set each pick in place.

WEAVING SMOOTH SELVEDGES

Achieving smooth selvedges can be a challenge. You might find it easy to do with one yarn, but then you switch to another and selvedge threads fray and break. The best way to avoid broken selvedge threads is to allow sufficient weft angle in the shed. Draw-in is the primary cause of broken selvedge threads. Practice consistency in placing the weft for each pick.

Crème de la Crème Poncho

DESIGN NOTES

A nice surprise when I finished this poncho is that it can be worn two ways: with the textured section along the shoulders and the braided fringes along the bottom or with the textured section down the center front and back, braids along the sides, and the plain selvedges along the bottom. Worn the latter way, the textured section forms a lovely focal point down the front of the body. You can weave the poncho in two panels on a narrower loom (see page 98). In either case, an option is to shape the neck opening on the loom (see page 103 for directions).

This is the only garment in this collection that isn't woven in plain weave. Based on the results of sampling, plain weave doesn't offer enough "oomph," but basketweave, while still a very simple structure, allows the textured wefts to show. The heavy texturing created by the finger-crocheted chains in the shoulder area balances the thick braids along the bottom edges. (The thick braids are achieved by adding threads to the fringe before braiding.)

EQUIPMENT

4-shaft loom, 50" weaving width for weaving the poncho in a single piece, 25" weaving width for weaving the poncho in two panels; 8-dent reed or rigid heddle; 3 rug shuttles; 1 boat shuttle; size G (4.5 m) crochet hook; size 10½ (6.5 mm) 24" circular knitting needle; tapestry needle.

MATERIALS

Warp 2-ply wool (900 yd/lb, 1,816 m/kg, Harrisville Highland, Harrisville Designs), White #44, 1,000 yd (yarn **W**).

Weft Wool roving (130 yd/100 g skein, 595 yd/lb, 1,200 m/kg, Montana, Tahki-Stacy Charles), Natural #01 (yarn **R**), 180 yd. Bouclé blend (54% mohair, 23% silk, 18% wool, 390 yd/8 oz skein, 780 yd/lb, 1,575 m/kg, Nantucket, Henry's Attic), Natural (yarn **B**), 122 yd (used doubled). Wool novelty (100% wool, 154 yd/8 oz skein, 308 yd/lb, 622 m/kg, Mikado, Henry's Attic), Natural (yarn **N**), 128 yd. 2-ply wool, White #44 (yarn **W**), 15 yd.

Other About 45 yd of each weft yarn for crocheted chain; about 30 yd of each weft yarn for braiding; about 30 yd wool roving for knitted neck ribbing; matching sewing thread.

WARP MEASUREMENTS

Total warp ends 400.

Warp length 2½ yd (allows for take-up, shrinkage, and 27" loom waste).

SETTS

EPI 8.
PPI 6⅓ (4½ in the shoulder/neck area).

FABRIC MEASUREMENTS

Width in reed 49¾".

Width after washing 40".

Woven length (measured under tension on the loom) 43" for poncho fabric plus 7" for waste-yarn sections at each end (57" total).

Length after washing 40" plus 7" waste-yarn sections at each end.

Take-up and shrinkage 20% in width, 12% in length.

Preparing the Weft

Before beginning to weave, using the three weft yarns together as a single yarn (1 strand roving, 1 strand bouclé, 1 strand wool novelty), prepare 18 finger-crocheted chains 22–24" long each as shown in Finger-Crocheting a Chain, page 97.

When you join wefts during weaving, use wet splicing for the roving (see Wet Splicing, page 93). Refer to the Checkered Sweater, pages 76–77, for detailed cut-and-sew instructions for neckline.

Weaving

Wind a warp of 400 ends White wool. Use your preferred method to warp the loom for plain weave; sley the 8-dent reed or rigid heddle 1/dent except sley the first and last 2 ends in a single dent (or slot or hole).

Use a boat shuttle for the White wool and wind a rug shuttle with each of the other yarns (R = roving, B = bouclé, N = novelty).

Following the treadling in the Poncho Draft, spread the warp in plain weave with a smooth nonfulling waste yarn (see Using Waste Yarn, page 15) for 7" and

Poncho Draft

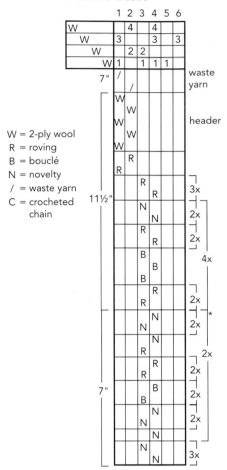

W = 2-ply wool
R = roving
B = bouclé
N = novelty
/ = waste yarn
C = crocheted chain

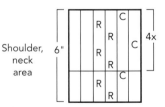

Shoulder, neck area

After completing the neck area follow the treadling above in reverse.

then continue weaving following the treadling in the draft. Note the length in woven inches that each section of the treadling should produce.

Shoulder section and neck opening: Using a neck template for the size of the desired opening and a washable sewing chalk, mark the neck opening on the warp threads. Raise shaft 1 and, using your fingers, insert a finger-crocheted chain from one selvedge to the edge of the marked neck opening. Leave a 2–3" tail at the selvedge to bring up into the next shed for the crocheted chain. Take another chain and insert it from the other selvedge to the neck opening, leaving a tail in the same way. Weave 2 picks of basketweave across the whole fabric with R. Always keep the chained yarn underneath the web as you weave the basketweave picks so that the turns of the chain are on the underside of the fabric. Raise shaft 3, insert the chain the same way, and follow with 2 picks basketweave. Repeat this process until you have woven 9 crochet-chain wefts (about 6"); end with 2 picks basketweave with R. The neck opening should now be completed (note that only the roving weaves inside the neck opening). Repeat the treadling sequences that you wove before the neck opening in reverse order for the other side of the poncho, ending with 7" plain weave with waste yarn.

FINGER CROCHETING A CHAIN

1 Holding 1 strand of each of the three weft yarns together, make a beginning loop.

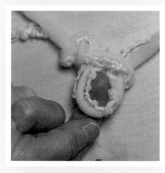

2 Insert your index finger through the loop and pull all 3 strands through the loop to form a new loop. These loops are large and chain-like in appearance.

3 Continue pulling a new loop through the old loop, sliding the old loop off your finger.

4 When the chain is the desired length, bring the ends of the yarn through the loop to tighten.

Washing

Remove the fabric from the loom, allowing enough warp beyond the waste-yarn areas for temporary knots to secure the waste yarn in place for washing. Tie loose knots in the fringe at both ends and machine wash with a mild detergent on a gentle cycle in warm water with a warm rinse for about 20 minutes (note that this amount of agitation works with my front-loading washer; make adjustments for your machine; see Washing, pages 118–119). Lay flat to dry. Steam lightly (see Steaming vs Pressing, page 120).

Assembly and Sewing
Mark the neck opening by handsewing with a basting thread; cut out the opening close to the basting thread. After cutting, remove the basting thread and machine zigzag around the neckline to secure the raw edge (see the Checkered Sweater, pages 76–77, for more details).

Using a size G crochet hook and the roving yarn (R), work a single crochet foundation row to cover the sewn edge as well as form a base for the neck ribbing (see Crocheted Edgings, page 122). Continue single crocheting for 68 stitches around the neckline to where you began, cut the yarn, and draw the end through the final loop. Weave in ends. This completes the foundation row to begin knitting the ribbed neckline.

NECK RIBBING

Using a size 10½ circular knitting needle and the roving yarn, pick up 1 stitch under each single crochet until you have 68 stitches on the needle. Join to work circularly. Work in k2, p2 ribbing until the band measures 2" or the desired length. Bind off stitches loosely. Weave in end. If there is any gap showing around the neckline where the edging meets the woven fabric, using a tapestry needle and a strand of roving (R), needleweave into the gap areas.

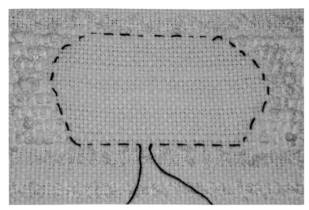

Mark the neck opening with a basting stitch.

BRAIDED FRINGE

Remove the waste yarn from the raw edges. Steam with a fabric steamer or iron (see Steaming vs Pressing, page 120) and then comb out the fringe warp ends. Weave a basting thread from selvedge to selvedge just above the 3rd pick of plain-weave header at both ends. The basting thread will guide you for inserting the extra yarns to add bulk to the fringe before braiding. Work the braids following the instructions in Braided Fringe.

On the wrong side, needleweave any tails from the crochet-chain weft for a few inches into an adjoining weft row.

Finish by steaming the poncho with a fabric steamer or an iron as above.

OTHER OPTIONS

If you have a narrow loom, the poncho can be woven in two panels and seamed. Use a warp width of 25" and a warp length of at least 3½ yd and follow weaving instructions for both panels. You can choose to leave an opening (a slit) in the center seam for the neckline in typical poncho fashion or you can treat the neckline the same way as for this one: Mark half of the neck opening and weave the crocheted chain from one selvedge to the marked opening only.

BRAIDED FRINGE

1 Hold 1 strand of each of the three weft yarns together and wind 20 times around two warping pegs 14" apart. Cut at both ends to make sixty 14" strands (you'll need more than these, but you can wind more when you run out).

2 Using a crochet hook and starting at one raw edge, insert the hook in the space between the 3rd and 4th warp threads from the selvedge in the weft row just below the row with the basting thread. Pull one 14" strand through so that two 7" pieces extend from the cloth.

3 Continue working across the edge, using R, B, N in sequence, pulling a strand through the fabric after every 3rd or 4th warp thread. Wind and cut additional 14" pieces as needed. Remove the basting thread.

4 To braid the fringe: Divide the fringe into 20 sections of about 2" each. You will make a standard 3-strand braid, but each "strand" is a group of yarns. Divide the 2" section into three groups. *Lay the right group over the middle group. The right group becomes the new middle group. Lay the left group over the new middle group.* Repeat between * for 7 crossings. The braid will be fluffy and full.

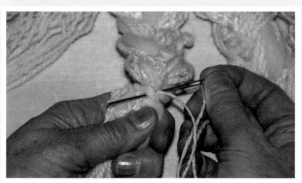

5 Wrap the end of the braid tightly with a strand of Highland wool about 18" long. Thread the tail of Highland into a tapestry needle, wind around the wrapping a few times, and take the needle in through the braid to bind off. Trim the tail flush with the braid. Repeat for each braid and then repeat the entire process on the other end of the poncho. Trim the ends of the braids evenly (the braids should be about 5" long).

6 Steam, trim, and lightly fluff the ends of the braids with your fingers.

Loopy Tabard

DESIGN NOTES

A singles handspun yarn with a lovely bumpy texture makes it a natural for forming weft loops that fluff open in the yoke of this vest. It also self-plies in such a way that creating a twisted side fringe with it is very easy— and fun—to do. The contrast in textures between the pile areas and the plain-weave areas is a delight to see and touch, and the simple go-anywhere garment can be worn with jeans, dressier pants, or skirt.

EQUIPMENT

2-shaft loom, 4-shaft loom, or rigid-heddle loom, 22" weaving width; 6-dent reed or rigid heddle; 3 boat or stick shuttles; 2 small stick shuttles; size E (3.5 m) crochet hook; tapestry needle.

MATERIALS

Warp 2-ply wool (900 yd/lb, 1,816 m/kg, Harrisville Highland, Harrisville Designs), Camel #42, 335 yd.

Weft 2-ply wool, Camel #42, 270 yd. 100% handspun, hand-dyed wool (110 yd/100 g, 505 yd/lb, 1,015 m/kg, Muench Yarns, Naturwolle, Black Forest Yarn), Crème #T1-41 and Camel #T1-41, about 220 yd each.

Other Heavyweight paper (large enough for making neck template).

Sometimes, all it takes is seeing a picture (or several) in a fashion magazine to inspire a new design. From a photo of a contemporary tabard-style vest and a separate photo of a collar made of twisted fringe, the design for this Loopy Tabard was born. The tabard is woven in one piece. The neckline shaping is done on the loom but finished off the loom with a crocheted edging. The Phillippine edging along the bottom is worked off the loom, and the twisted-cord closures are added last.

WARP MEASUREMENTS

Total warp ends 134.

Warp length 2½ yd (allows for take-up, shrinkage, and 27" loom waste).

SETTS

EPI 6.
PPI 8.

FABRIC MEASUREMENTS

Width in reed 22".

Width after washing 18½".

Woven length (measured under tension on the loom) 56".

Length after washing 48" total (24" for front and 24" for back).

Take-up and shrinkage 15% in width and length.

Weft Color Order

Weaving

Wind a warp of 134 ends Camel Highland wool. Use your preferred method to warp the loom for plain weave, sleying 1/dent in a 6-dent reed or heddle (except sley the first and last 2 ends in a single dent but thread them in separate heddles if you are using a shaft loom), and center for 22". Tie the warp onto the front apron rod.

Spread the warp by weaving a 2" header using waste yarn. Starting at the bottom edge of the front panel and using Camel Highland wool, weave ¾" of plain weave, beating firmly so that the fabric is almost weft-faced (this will be a bottom border). Then weave plain weave at 8 picks per inch following the Weft Color Order for 18".

The yoke features weft-pile loops with a twisted-fringe edging at the shoulders; both the loops and the edging are done with only the handspun yarn. For the next 5", make the twisted side fringe and weft-pile loops using both colors of the handspun yarn (see Twisted Side Fringe and Weft-Pile Loops, page 103).

The front panel will now measure about 24" from the beginning. At this point, start the neck opening. Make a neckline template following directions on page 61.

Place the template in the center of the warp and using a marker, draw the outline on the warp threads and mark the top shoulderline; see page 104. Then, using 2 small flat shuttles with Camel Highland wool and 4 yarn butterflies (2 of each color of the handspun yarn), continue weaving on both sides of the marked neck opening, making the weft pile and twisted side fringe with the handspun. When you reach the top shoulderline, measure from the 1st pick of weft loops to the top shoulderline (about 9" total for mine). Finish the neck opening, change back to the original shuttles, and weave selvedge to selvedge with weft loops on the back panel so that the distance from the top shoulderline to the last row of weft loops is the same as you measured for the yoke on the front panel.

Then weave the body of the back panel below the yoke (without making fringe and loops) following the Weft Color Order in reverse for 18". Weave ¾" with Camel Highland wool beaten firmly as at the beginning and end with 2" of plain weave in waste yarn; remove the fabric from the loom.

TWISTED SIDE FRINGE

The twisted fringe along the selvedges of the yoke is simpler to make than it looks because the handspun does most of the work for you. Instead of turning the handspun weft around the selvedge threads as for the Highland, bring it out about 2" and fold it before taking it back into the web, leaving a 2" folded loop of fringe beyond the selvedge. The singles yarn in the loop will twist on itself (you can always add more twist if desired before folding it).

Assembly and Sewing
NECK OPENING

To make a firm edge for the neckline that frames the handspun and mimics the knotted edging around the bottom of the tabard, a row of single crochet is worked around the unwoven warp threads in the neck opening before the ends are needlewoven back into the neckline; see Finishing the Neckline Edge, page 105.

Using a crochet hook, work single crochet (see Crocheted Edgings, page 122) around each warp thread to secure the neck edge. Place the hook under the warp thread and pull the crochet loop around the warp thread, before moving on to the next thread. After crocheting completely around the neckline, push the crocheted chain snug against the weft.

WEFT-PILE LOOPS

To form the weft loops, when you are weaving with the Crème and Camel handspun yarn, use your fingers to pull the weft into ½–¾" loops 1–2" apart between pairs of warp threads, staggering the spacing of the loops from row to row.

Cut across the open warp threads in the middle of the neck opening. Needleweave each cut warp end back into the cloth for about 1½", following the path of the adjacent warp thread on the back side of the fabric.

BOTTOM EDGING

Remove the waste yarn and place the garment on a table with the wrong side of one bottom edge facing toward you. To make the Phillippine edge (see page 105): Starting at the left, hold the first 2 warp threads taut—these are passive threads. With the 3rd warp end, tie a half hitch around the passive strands. Drop the 1st passive strand and add the tail of the 3rd strand to the left hand. Pick up the next warp end to the right and tie a half hitch around the 2 strands now in your left hand. Continue across the row, using the next warp thread to the right to tie a half hitch around the 2 strands at the left. When you are finished tying the fringe, using a tapestry needle, needleweave each warp end along the path of the adjacent warp end as for the neckline. Trim ends.

TIES

Measure and cut 8 strands Camel Highland wool 40" long. Along one selvedge for the length of tabard fabric, measure 6" from a bottom edge and, using a tapestry needle or crochet hook, bring 2 of these strands through the fabric 2 warp ends inside the selvedge. Pull the strands halfway through the cloth and then take the ends of 2 strands in each of your hands. Twist both pairs clockwise until they start to kink. Take all 4 strands in one hand and keeping them under tension, allow them to twist around themselves, guiding them as they twist. Secure the end with a knot; trim. Repeat this for the opposite selvedge at the same end of the fabric and then again for both selvedges at the opposite end.

Washing

The final washing is done after the assembly and finishes are complete so that the entire garment, including the ties, shrinks evenly. Handwash in warm water with a mild detergent; rinse in warm water. (Handwashing will make sure that softly spun yarns don't felt or fray, which could occur in the machine.) Lay flat to dry.

WEAVING THE NECKLINE OPENING

Place the template under the warp so the neck opening shows.

Draw the outline on the warp threads and remove the template.

Weave with separate wefts on each side of the opening.

FINISHING THE NECKLINE EDGE

Single crochet around each warp thread along the neckline edge.

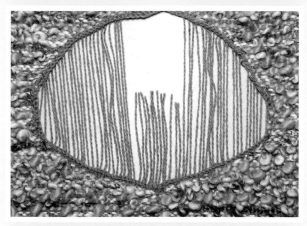

Cut across the warp threads in the middle of the opening.

Needleweave each warp thread back into the cloth.

WORKING A PHILLIPPINE EDGE

Tie a half hitch around threads 1 and 2 with thread 3.

After tying them all, needleweave warp threads into the edge.

Trim the warp tails flush with the cloth.

Wabi Sabi Jacket

Japanese indigo cloth inspired this fabric, as did the simplicity of Japanese design. I let a "wabi sabi" aesthetic—welcoming the imperfect and the asymmetrical—take over during the weaving process. The fabric is woven with irregular density in weft stripes by tripling the weft in areas, and one vest front is fringed, while the other is not. The planning of the jacket layout was intentional, however, to produce a simple garment with a relaxed, organic feel and to weave all the pieces on one warp.

DESIGN NOTES

First, I made a muslin sample for size and fit. You can modify the sizing for yourself (see Making a Sample Garment, pages 58–59). Next came the planning of the warp layout. The sleeves and back are woven first and then the warp threads on one side are dropped to weave the narrower front pieces, one at a time. This causes extra waste of warp yarn, but using a separate, narrower warp for these two pieces would create loom waste, too, plus take additional time to wind.

You can wear this jacket with one front overlapping the other with a pin closure or you can add buttons. Only the overlapping (right) front edge of this jacket is fringed, but if you want to wear the jacket open and have fringe along both front edges, you can weave it on both.

EQUIPMENT

2-shaft loom, 4-shaft loom, or rigid-heddle loom, 27" weaving width; 12-dent reed or rigid heddle; 4 shuttles.

MATERIALS

Warp 2-ply wool (1,800 yd/lb, 3,630 m/kg, Harrisville Shetland, Harrisville Designs) Charcoal #49, 1,620 yd.

Weft 2-ply wool, Charcoal #49, Midnight Blue #3, and Silver Mist #53, about 1,200 yd total (about 500 yd of Silver Mist and 350 yd each of Charcoal and Midnight Blue for this jacket).

Other Butcher paper for making a sleeve template; tapestry needle; T-pins; matching sewing thread.

WARP MEASUREMENTS

Total warp ends 324.

Warp length 5 yd (allows for take-up, shrinkage, and 25" loom waste).

SETTS

EPI 12.
PPI 12.

FABRIC MEASUREMENTS

Width in reed 27".

Width after washing 23" for the back and sleeve pieces; 13½" for each of the two front pieces, not including side fringe.

Woven length (measured under tension on the loom) 142" (2" waste-yarn section, 28" back, 3" waste-yarn section, 28" front, 3" waste-yarn section, 28" front, 3" waste-yarn section, 21" sleeve, 3" waste-yarn section, 21" sleeve, 2" waste-yarn section).

Length after washing 127½" (1¾" waste-yarn section, 24" back, 2½" waste-yarn section, 24" front, 2½" waste-yarn section, 24" front, 2½" waste-yarn section, 21" sleeve, 2½" waste-yarn section, 21" sleeve, 1¾" waste-yarn section).

Length after sewing From shoulder seam to bottom of fringe 25"; sleeve length is 18", including fringe.

Take-up and shrinkage 15% in width and length.

Preparing the Weft

Three weft colors are used to weave weft stripes of random sizes and in random order. All stripes in this jacket are wider than ½" and narrower than 1¾". One shuttle is wound with 3 strands of Silver Mist wool, the other 3 shuttles with 1 strand each of Silver Mist, Charcoal, and Midnight Blue. In the stripes of Silver Mist, the 3-strand shuttle is used predominantly, except occasionally a single strand is interspersed to add textural variety. You can modify this plan any way you desire.

Weaving

Wind a warp of 324 ends of Charcoal wool. Use your preferred method to warp the loom for plain weave, sleying 1/dent in a 12-dent reed (or rigid heddle) and centering for 27". Tie the warp onto the front apron rod.

Spread the warp with a 2" header using a smooth, nonfulling waste yarn (see Using Waste Yarn, page 15). Weave the first sleeve with random striping for 21"; see the Layout, page 111). End with 3" using waste yarn. Repeat for the second sleeve. Next, weave the back, continuing random striping for 28"; end with 3" in waste yarn.

Cut 108 warp threads, leave 4, cut 20 to weave the fronts.

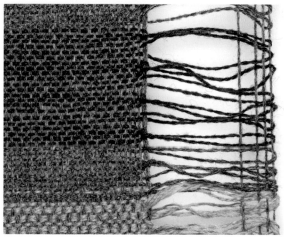

The 4 warp threads remaining are a "selvedge" for side fringe.

To prepare the warp for the narrower front pieces: Starting at the right side of the warp at least 6" beyond the fell, cut 108 warp threads (9" weaving width). Secure the weft at the fell by tying temporary square knots in 1" groups of the cut warp threads close to the last pick of waste yarn. Pull the other ends of the cut threads out of the heddles and suspend them from the back beam. Leave the next 4 warp threads

in place and then cut and secure the next 20 warp threads in the same way as for the others (the 4 uncut warp threads will be used to catch the weft for a side fringe). You now have 16" of warp width remaining on the loom, not including the 4 warp threads beyond the 20-thread gap.

CREATING TEXTURE

You can create various thicknesses of wefts with the same weft yarn by winding multiple strands of weft together. With a lightweight weft, you'll need at least 3 weft strands to make enough contrast with a single strand.

Now weave the right front jacket piece. Make a plain-weave shed and take the shuttle into the shed from left to right, bringing it out in the space between the cloth warp and the 4 extra warp threads. Then make the next shed and take the shuttle back to the left selvedge. Change the shed and weave from left to right through the shed in the main fabric and also through the shed formed by the 4 extra warp threads. Change the shed again and weave back to the left selvedge. Repeat this process to weave the first front piece for 28".

When you finish the first front piece, weave 3" with waste yarn and then cut the 4 warp threads you used to create the fringe in the same way as you cut the others, securing them against the fell, and weave the left front piece without the side fringe for 28". (If you want fringe on the edges of both front pieces, leave

the 4 warp threads in place. The fabric is reversible, so it doesn't matter that the fringe on both pieces is woven on the same side; it can be flipped for constructing the garment.)

After the left front is completed, end with about 2" of waste yarn to secure the edge and then remove the fabric from the loom, allowing 4" or so of warp length beyond the last waste-yarn picks for tying temporary knots.

Washing

Tie loose knots in the warp threads at both raw edges of the fabric to secure the waste yarn for wet-finishing. Machine wash with a mild detergent on a gentle cycle in warm water with a warm rinse for about 28 minutes (note that this amount of agitation works with my front-loading washer; make adjustments for your machine; see Washing, pages 118–119). Lay flat to dry. Remove the waste yarn. Steam using a fabric steamer or an iron (see Steaming vs Pressing, page 120).

Remove the 4 warp threads from the fringe area on the right front piece. Separate the pieces by cutting the warp threads through the center of the sections where you removed the waste yarn; the cut warp ends will become the fringe (on the bottom of the sleeves and the jacket and around the neckline) and will be about 1¼" long. Label each fabric piece (sleeves, back, right front, left front) to make construction easier.

Assembly and Sewing
SLEEVES

Make a sleeve template following the diagram on page 111. Cut each sleeve according to template. Using a pin or thread marker, mark the shoulder seams on the top fronts and the back for 7" from the selvedges. Machine zigzag the raw edges at the top of the sleeve pieces (the 23" edge) and along the marked 7" areas on the fronts and back. Trim the warp fringe beyond the machine zigzagging to about ½". Trim the bottom fringes of the sleeves, back, and fronts to even them (about ¾" or so in length). Trim to leave the same length of fringe (or as desired) along the side of the right front piece. Brush all fringes to fluff them and brush the bottom edges toward the cloth to secure them.

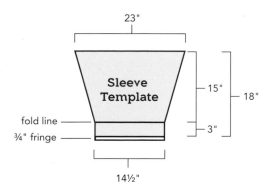

Sleeve Template

23"

15"

18"

fold line

¾" fringe

3"

14½"

SHOULDER SEAMS

Use matching Shetland wool yarn for all seams. With right sides together, pin the front pieces to the back along the shoulders. Backstitch (see page 121) the shoulder seams between the 2nd and 3rd weft rows. Lightly steam the seams open.

Open the garment and lay it flat, right sides up. Place the sleeves so the top of the shoulder is aligned with the center of the top of the sleeve and mark the sleeve positions on the garment. Pin sleeves to the garment, right sides together. Backstitch to seam the sleeves to the fronts and back. Lightly steam seams open.

With right sides together, fold the garment at the shoulders, and for each sleeve, pin the underarm sleeve seam and then backstitch from the underarm to the sleeve bottom, reversing the seam by back-stitching on the right side of the fabric in the last 3" to form a cuff. With right sides together, pin and then backstitch both side seams.

Steam all seams. Note that you can brush the entire fabric, but do so before cutting and sewing (see Brushing, pages 119–120). You can also make the fringe longer or have no fringe at all, but in that case you will need to finish the edges by hemming or some other edge treatment.

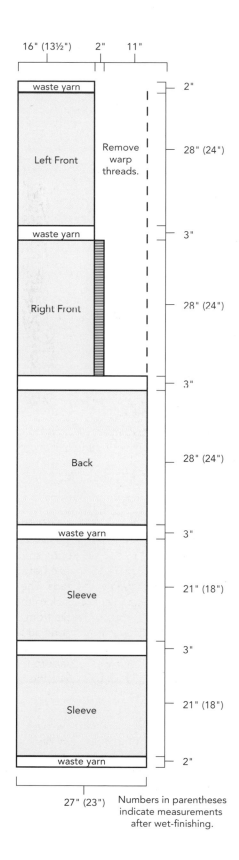

16" (13½")   2"   11"

waste yarn — 2"

Left Front   Remove warp threads.   28" (24")

waste yarn — 3"

Right Front   28" (24")

— 3"

Back   28" (24")

waste yarn — 3"

Sleeve   21" (18")

— 3"

Sleeve   21" (18")

waste yarn — 2"

27" (23")   Numbers in parentheses indicate measurements after wet-finishing.

Liz Spear
WORKING COLLABORATIVELY

The idea of working collaboratively with fellow artists for my garment line came along in 1999, when I started sharing my craft fair booth with another weaver, Neal Howard. At the time, she was exclusively weaving scarves and wraps using her hand-dyed silk yarn. Her accessories dovetailed nicely with my garments, and soon a marketing partnership ensued; we still exhibit at craft fairs together.

At some point, she began giving me the woven ends of her scarf warps, and I got the idea of incorporating them into some of my garments. These collaborative pieces were the most exciting garments in the booth, sparking much discourse with customers.

Two years later, Laura Sims, a master marbler, announced she was writing a book on marbling and invited several fiber artists to collaborate with her on pieces for the gallery section. She marbled part of one of my handwoven garments, thoroughly enhancing the colors of the yarn and the lines of the garment. We decided that this collaboration was destined to continue, and now I work with her in her studio, participating in all the steps.

Over the past ten years, I've worked with a landscape quilter from Alabama; a paper artist from Tennessee, who wanted to wear a paper coat to her son's wedding; and a knitter/spinner from nearby, who was interested in combining knitting and weaving. Catharine Ellis, my friend, mentor, and teacher, has contributed a number of shibori-woven fabrics, as have other local handweavers. Every one of these collaborations has expanded my knowledge and experience.

PHOTOS BY MARY VOGEL

Each of the collaborative garments begins with the other fiber artist's work—on the cutting table. I react to the color, the texture, the thought of my friend's smile as she works in her studio/dyepot/marbling tray, and I begin to audition my own fabrics. I look for color and value relationships, using contrast and complements to create a beautiful and interesting composition. Sometimes the "match" is immediate; sometimes I'll keep trying different combinations.

My most recent collaborations involve my making pieces of nuno felt—combining fine merino wool with woven silk fabrics dyed or painted by other artists. I'm also combining nuno fabric with my handwoven cloth, which is spurring all kinds of new ideas.

Every collaborator is noted on the garment hang-tag, and a special label is sewn in, "LIZ SPEAR & FRIENDS," which itself sparks interest and conversation.

Working collaboratively has enriched my creative and business life immeasurably. If you want to consider it yourself, think about how you work. Then look for someone whose skills dovetail with yours and whose work you admire. I suggest you both create two pieces, one for each of you, whether weaving cloth, dyeing or painting, sewing garments, or embellishing, and then decide whether it's a fit.

LIZ SPEAR completed her BFA in ceramics at St. Cloud State University in Minnesota in 1977. After working as a potter for thirteen years, she moved to western North Carolina and studied under Catharine Ellis at Haywood Community College. She is now a full-time studio artist, marketing through professional craft organizations, and she teaches at various national craft schools.

Elizabeth Jenkins

I started my textile journey in the early 1970s. I fell in love with the weaving traditions of Oaxaca, Mexico, and Guatemala, learning backstrap weaving in Guatemala from an amazing Indian woman. Guatemala was the beginning of my love of vibrant colors and indigenous cultures. From there I traveled and lived in South America, staying the longest in Bolivia, and started collecting textiles. It was also at this time that I met a gypsy who foretold my production-weaving future. Over the years I have traveled to Indonesia, Morocco, Turkey, India, Laos, Thailand, Vietnam, and Japan—all countries with strong textile traditions.

Although I had learned weaving fundamentals a few years earlier, it wasn't until my move to northern New Mexico in 1978 that I bought my first loom. At first, I favored colonial overshot but soon realized that for me, weaving was all about color and texture and garment making. This realization fit perfectly with being in New Mexico with its bright sun and blue sky. I have no formal training in the arts but have attended many surface design conferences and taken classes in different techniques from around the world.

I favor the cellulose fibers of cotton and rayon and the protein ones of silk, alpaca, mohair, and wool in my weavings. The warps I make in wool and mohair are usually more neutral in coloring than the silk and cotton warps are, but all have some variegation. My woven structure is a simple plain weave, with most of the emphasis coming from the weft.

PHOTOS BY CLAY ELLIS

What is important
to me is the graphic
clarity of the design.

I am most interested in creating cloth that seems to
take on a quality of multidimensionality and layering.
With the use of a silk screen and discharge paste,
I add pattern to the surface of the weaving. The
process of taking dye out of the yarns produces color
variations that are visually complex. Many of the symbols and designs I favor seem to be either Japanese
or North American. What is important to me is the
graphic clarity of the design.

I can see the influence of various textiles traditions
from around the world in my work. I surround myself
with textiles from all these places and stand in awe of
human accomplishment.

As a self-taught weaver, **ELIZABETH
JENKINS** has formed a creative process that is
very intuitive and nonlinear; her sense of color
and contrast comes from her connections to
indigenous cultures. She continues to travel,
study, and collect textiles worldwide.

Teri D. Inman

Using my imagination to create things with my hands has been a lifelong passion. Since 1976, I have immersed myself in the fiber arts and have developed a successful business making and marketing my handwoven designs. Complex colors and simple but elegant designs are the foundation of this success.

KYLE INMAN

In the design process, I focus on garments that have a fluid drape and clean lines and are attractive on a variety of body shapes and sizes. The simplicity of the garment allows the yarns, weave structure, and colors to be showcased.

Silk and cashmere have become my chosen yarns—a silk warp provides stability, fluidity, and luster, and a cashmere weft (or sometimes fine wools and alpaca) provides an unparalleled softness and contrasting matte finish.

After experimenting with many weave structures, I find twills provide the best drape and versatility in design, particularly turned-twill block weaves, with the many variations in threading, tie-up, and treadling orders that they provide.

> The simplicity of the garment allows the yarns, weave structure, and colors to be showcased.

RICK INMAN

MICHAEL LEWIS

KYLE INMAN

I use specialized dye processes to produce a medley of color blends: variegated weft yarns, warp painting, handpainted fabrics, and my own variation of arashi shibori. In arashi shibori, the cloth is wrapped on a diagonal around a pole. A thread is wound very tightly around the cloth on the pole, and the cloth is compressed and then dyed. The result is a pleated cloth with a design on a diagonal. Pleating on silk, which is the traditional fabric, is not permanent. In addition, I learned to appreciate the wonderful characteristics of animal fibers, such as wool, cashmere, and alpaca. These fibers will hold a shape after being subjected to changes in temperature and agitation and therefore maintain the pleating.

My garment designs have evolved through years of experimentation. Scarves and shawls and the simple shape of the quechquemitl and ruana are my basics along with jackets and vests based on variations of the classic kimono shape. Most of my garments use the same warp width, so one long warp can produce many different styles. Garment design is a continuing process of research, experimentation, and listening to the wonderful people who are my customers.

TERI D. INMAN sells her designer originals exclusively through her studio Bristol Yarnworks Studio in Creede, Colorado, and at selected events. Teri designs, weaves, owns, and operates The Yarn Shoppe and teaches workshops.

CHAPTER 6

Finishing

Finishing a garment involves more than just wet-finishing the fabric. It also includes garment construction, closures, edge treatments, and embellishments.

Washing

Of all the steps in creating a handwoven piece, from yarn choices to the weaving process, it's the washing of the fabric that can make or break the final project. Most woven fabric for clothing needs to be washed, either by hand or in the washing machine, so the yarns can relax and bloom. For wool fabrics, washing is critical for fulling.

You can machine wash fabric in either a front-loading or a top-loading washer. My preference is a front loader because it doesn't agitate the fabric as much as a top loader does. Because of this, the washing time in a front loader must generally be longer than in a top loader to achieve the same degree of agitation. No matter what type of machine you use, first test

out the water temperature and number of minutes of agitation with a sample.

A top-loading washing machine does allow for stopping and starting the cycle, giving you more control over timing. Always check your wool fabric after 5 minutes of agitation and then again every 2 to 3 minutes. For garments, you usually want wool to full enough to become soft; you should see a slight fuzzing on the surface. You don't want a stiff fabric or a felt-like texture for most garments.

If you are using a top loader and your cloth is longer than 2 yards with waste at the ends, baste the ends together to form a continuous circle to promote equal fulling over the entire piece. (In the case of fringed ends on projects, temporarily tie the ends in 1–2"

Harrisville Designs wool woven in twill. From left to right: Unprocessed, handwashed, fulled in washing machine.

Harrisville Designs wool brushed on one side.

groups of warp threads.) Distribute the cloth evenly around the agitator to avoid twisting and knotting.

A tightly woven fabric will shrink much less than a loosely woven one, yet the fibers in the loosely woven one will bloom more, thus creating a softer hand. Woolen-spun Harrisville Design yarns can shrink as much as 20%, depending on the degree of fulling and warp and weft density.

Three factors cause woolen fabric to full (or if taken to the extreme, to become felt-like).

❖ **Agitation provided by machine or by hand**
If you want a felt-like result by hand, you'll need to do much rubbing and pummeling.

❖ **Water with detergent** Use a mild, environmentally friendly detergent with a neutral pH and lots of water. (I use Orvus Paste, 100% sodium lauryl sulfate—it contains no dyes, perfumes, fats, oils, enzymes, or brighteners. It can be used in cold, warm, or hot water, dissolves quickly, and rinses away cleanly without leaving a residue. It's used to clean livestock, so I purchase mine at a feed store in a large 7½ lb jug. It lasts for years because it's very concentrated.)

❖ **Temperature control** Wool needs warm water, 100° to 120°F at the warmest. The hotter the water, the more the yarn will fuzz. If you want a felt-like texture, shock the fabric by switching between very hot and very cold water. Remember, you can

always full a fabric more, but you can't take away fulling that has occurred. Handwash when you want minimal shrinkage and lightly knead the fabric. You'll need a bathtub or large basin and lots of water for sufficient fabric movement. When you are washing silk, use warm water, 100° to 110°F, air dry partially, and then steam-press, covering with a towel first. Treat cotton the same way.

Allow the fabric to air-dry on a flat surface. The flat surface can be a bed or a table or floor space covered with towels. Wherever you lay your fabric to dry, make sure that the surface is clean and the towels don't have any coloring that can bleed into the cloth. Drying time will vary, but if you plan to brush a wool fabric to raise the nap, brush while it is still a bit damp.

Brushing

Brushing or raising the nap of the cloth creates a thick, warm fabric because it adds more air spaces for insulation. It also visually blends colors and softens fabric surfaces. Woven patterns can be obscured by brushing, so plain weave or simple twills are the best structures to use with a brushed surface. The nap on loosely spun or plied yarns raises more readily than on tightly spun ones, with wool and mohair being the best fibers for brushing.

If the fabric has dried, steam it or lightly spritz it with water for brushing. I usually steam an area, then brush it with a nylon-bristle brush. Brush with the grain, first in the warp direction and then, if you want more nap, in the weft direction. Be very careful not to allow the brushing to distort the cloth, particularly if the weave is loosely woven (such as for the Striped Mohair Shawl (page 43). If the project is not reversible, only one side may need to be brushed.

Steaming vs Pressing

I steam all my cloth and then steam the finished garment, too. Steaming relaxes the fibers after washing and drying. Any wrinkles or bumpy seams smooth with steaming. I use a professional fabric steamer because I haven't had luck with the less expensive hand-held ones on the market.

Steam the cloth while it's flat, moving the steamer along the surface. Let the cloth dry before moving on to your next finishing step (unless you're brushing it next). For a garment, you may want to steam the neck and shoulder seams with the garment on a dress form.

If you don't have a steamer, you can use a steam iron, but do not place the iron directly on the surface. Instead, hover the iron a few inches above the fabric so the cloth absorbs the steam. If the fabric requires pressing as well, which is sometimes necessary on seams, use a damp pressing cloth on top of the woven fabric.

Machine Sewing

Sewing is done for multiple purposes—to finish raw edges before washing before and/or after cutting the cloth, for seaming, and for some embellishing. All sewing can be done by hand, but using a machine does save time.

I use a sewing machine with handwovens only for machine zigzagging raw edges to prevent raveling. I do all other stitching by hand.

Use machine zigzagging to secure raw edges.

MACHINE ZIGZAGGING

Use a wide zigzag stitch with close spacing. Line up the machine footer so that the stitching goes over 2 picks or warp threads on light- and medium-weight fabrics. For heavier-weight fabrics, the stitching may not catch enough of the warp and weft threads, so two rows of zigzagging may be needed.

Handsewing

Sewing of garments can be done in so many ways that sometimes the stitches you use are simply a matter of personal choice. Invisible stitches can be used for joining panels; hemstitches for edges; and decorative stitches for edges, trims, and embroidered motifs.

INVISIBLE JOINING STITCH (ALSO CALLED INVISIBLE SEAM)

Place the two fabric pieces side by side and sew them together at the selvedges by joining every weft row or other spacing.

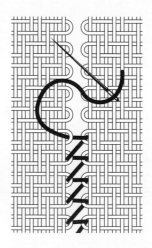

RUNNING STITCH

Pick up several warp or weft threads at a time on a needle (about ⅜" in length), go over the fabric surface about ⅜", and repeat.

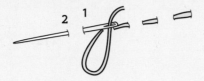

BACKSTITCH

For the projects in this book, a backstitch is used to seam two pieces of fabric placed right sides together with a seam allowance of ¼–⅜". Make a running stitch about ⅜" long, reinsert the needle at the end of the first stitch, bring it forward on the underside of the fabric, and bring it up through the surface one stitch length beyond the previous stitch. Repeat.

BUTTONHOLE STITCH

This is also known as blanket stitch. Working from right to left, anchor the yarn at the edge and *take the needle through the fabric from front to back, about ¼" below the edge. Pull the needle toward the edge with the yarn held in back of the needle. Repeat from * across the top of the work, spacing stitches evenly (close for buttonholes, farther apart or as desired for reinforcing other edges).

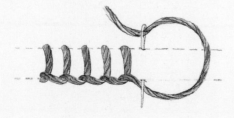

HEMSTITCHING

Weave plain weave, ending with the shuttle on the right side if you are right-handed or the left side if you are left-handed. Measure a length of weft three times the width of the warp and cut, leaving the measured length as a tail. Thread the tail into a blunt tapestry needle. Take the needle under a group of ends above the fell and bring it up and back to the starting point, encircling the group. Pass the needle under the same group of ends, bringing it out through the weaving 2 (or more) weft threads below the fell. Repeat for each group of ends across the fell. Needleweave the tail into the selvedge and trim.

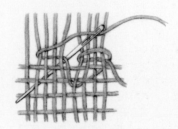

OVERCAST HEM STITCH

This is also known as slanting hem stitch. Insert the needle within the folded hem, bring it out of the fold at A and pick up a few threads at B close to the edge of the fold but a stitch length in front of A. Slanting the needle, slip the point under the edge of the fold at C so the distance from B to C is the same as from B to A.

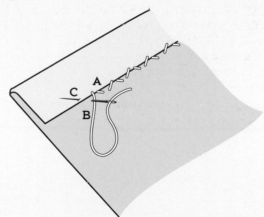

Crocheted Edgings

Simple crocheted edgings provide a clean finish or decorative edging for woven cloth. Crochet can also be used to join fabrics together once you know the single crochet stitch.

SINGLE CROCHET

Insert hook into a stitch, yarn over hook and draw up a loop (A), yarn over hook and draw it through both loops on hook (B).

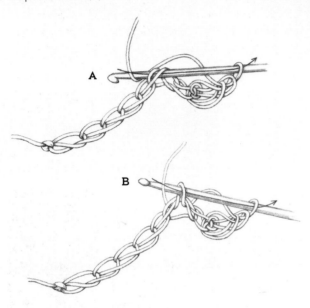

JOINING FABRICS USING SINGLE CROCHET

1. Insert the hook in the edge of the fabric (A). Holding the yarn in your left hand behind the fabric, with the hook in your right hand, catch the yarn with the hook and pull a loop though the fabric (B).

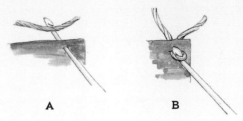

2. Catch the yarn with the hook (C); pull the loop through the first loop, sliding the first loop off the hook (D).

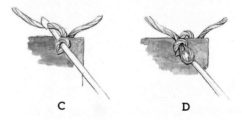

3. Insert the hook back into the fabric to begin the next single crochet. There are now two loops on the hook. Bring the yarn over the hook and draw a new loop through both loops on the hook.

Embellishments

Possible closures, edging, and embellishing treatments for woven cloth are without limit. Look at fashion, sewing, and knitting magazines for ideas. Closures are as simple as belts, buttons, hooks and eyes, decorative pins, snaps, tied cords, and more. Also consider cut buttonholes, knotted cords, and lacing. For surface-stitching ideas, refer to embroidery books; a few are noted in Resources, page 142. There are no limits to the ways you can add design elements to a garment.

Buttons

Good-quality, beautiful buttons are worth buying whenever you see them (I have a button stash along with a yarn stash!). Visit specialty button shops as well as secondhand and antiques stores. Buying a jar full of buttons at a flea market is very worthwhile if you find a few spectacular ones. Handwoven garments cry for special buttons.

The more patterned and complex the cloth, the simpler the button should be. The simpler the cloth, the fancier the button should be. Take your sample fabric with you when you are shopping for buttons so you can compare and contrast. I take other fabric swatches with me, too, for buttons for future projects.

You can make covered buttons, either with your handwoven cloth or a contrasting cloth, or you can crochet a cover.

Ties join the sides of the Loopy Tabard, page 104.

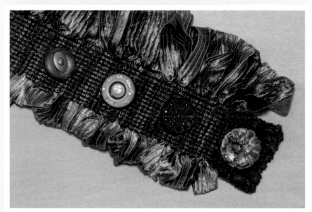

Buttons make ideal embellishments.

A button adds sparkle to the Ribbon Collar, page 23.

You can cover buttons with crochet or woven cloth.

Crocheted loops are an alternative to tailored buttonholes.

Use a spacer between the thread and the button (a wooden matchstick or toothpick works). Sew the button to the fabric and remove the spacer.

Bring the needle through the button but not the fabric. Wrap the thread around the thread between the button and the fabric several times, then take the needle through the fabric and secure it on the back.

If you don't want to cut into the cloth to make a buttonhole, sew the button onto the cloth, attach a snap on the wrong side of the cloth under the button, and sew the other half of the snap to the fabric edge to be joined.

Another option is crocheted buttonhole loops. Mark the button-loop placement. Starting at the edge of the fabric, work one row of single crochet across the entire fabric edge, turn. On the second row, work single crochet up to the marker for a button loop and then *crochet a chain long enough to accommodate your button. Attach the chain into the fabric with a single crochet, continue to the next marker, and repeat from * until the last loop is made. Finish crocheting across the fabric to the end.

When you are attaching a flat button that doesn't have a shank, you can make one as you sew the button to the fabric.

Surface and Edge Treatments

One of my favorite aspects of garment making is choosing an edge treatment. I love crocheting a seam instead of sewing it or finishing a neckline edge with a special stitch. For collars, cuffs, and necklines, I use knitted ribbing. Knitted strips can cover raw edges while providing a contrast that frames the piece.

SAMPLING different edge treatments is as important as all types of sampling. To do this, you need the woven samples you wet-finished when you were planning the piece. For the Striped Ruana sample, I tested out two different knitted edgings. Again, I hung the swatch at a distance to see the edging color against the woven cloth. I wanted the edging to blend with the fabric without too much contrast. The darker color worked best (see page 125).

FRINGING is a common edge treatment for the bottom of a garment and for the ends of scarves and shawls. What about augmenting the fringe? For the Crème de la Crème Poncho, I added yarn to the fringe and then braided it (page 99). For the Wabi Sabi Jacket, I created a side fringe (running in the weft direction on the loom) to add interest to the center front edge (page 109). For the Checkered Sweater, I took advantage of the washed fringe and used it at the neckline (page 76).

Single crochet can frame a piece and define its lines.

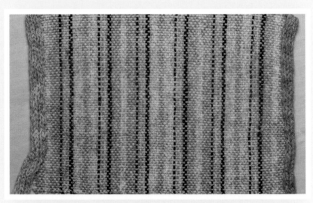

Use fabric samples to try out edgings.

Fringe can be braided and augmented for more texture.

A knitted ribbing creates a sturdy, decorative finished edge.

BRAIDING is another way to use thrums. A braided edging on any number of these projects would make an effective finish. Designer Heather Winslow (pages 136–137) takes braiding many steps beyond a 3-strand braid and uses kumihimo braiding for a lovely finish.

EMBROIDERING on the surface of a handwoven can add great design interest. A very simple flower is added to the Blooming Scarf (page 133). Beads can be added to fringe (see the Plaid Cowl, page 129) or to a fabric surface.

PIPING the woven edge of a collar is a great way to coordinate a top and a jacket or use up scraps of cloth. It also gives a very professional finish to the garment.

Simple embroidery can add just the right touch.

Plaid Cowl

DESIGN NOTES

With this laceweight mohair blend, 10 epi is an ideal warp sett (12 epi would work but produce a less airy fabric than this cowl). I used a boat shuttle, but note that mohair yarn can catch at the edges of the bobbin. Keep the bobbin rod free of mohair at all times. When you are winding the bobbin, don't overfill it.

You can weave this cowl as a tubular doubleweave using a nonsticky yarn. Instead of a seam, this would produce fringe on the top and bottom edges of the cowl. I didn't do it this way with the mohair because—well—it's mohair. Double the threads equals sticky issues for sure.

The first time I wove with mohair, I couldn't open a shed! The challenge in using mohair is that the little hairs typical of a brushed mohair yarn can stick to each other during the steps required for warping and weaving. But don't let this discourage you, because there are ways to prevent this from happening. Most important to keep in mind is that the warp needs to be sett more openly (fewer ends per inch) than the number you'd get by wrapping a ruler with the yarn in the usual way. The little hairs need room both for fulling during finishing and to be kept somewhat separate from each other during warping and weaving.

EQUIPMENT

2-shaft loom, 4-shaft loom, or rigid-heddle loom, 23" weaving width; 10-dent reed or rigid heddle; 1 shuttle.

MATERIALS

Warp Kid mohair/nylon blend (70% kid mohair, 30% nylon, 4,450 yd/lb, 8,980 m/kg, Kid Mohair Lace Weight, Louet), Silver #38, 257 yd; Dark Olive #41, 243 yd.

Weft Kid mohair/nylon blend: Dark Olive #41 and Silver #38, 150 yd each.

Other Glass beads (optional): For this cowl, twenty-eight ¼" beads are tied into the fringe, forty-four $3/16$–$5/16$" beads are sewn along the inside seam.

WARP MEASUREMENTS

Total warp ends 222 (see Warp Color Order).

Warp length 2¼ yd (allows for take-up, shrinkage, and 27" loom waste.

SETTS

EPI 10.
PPI 10.

FABRIC MEASUREMENTS

Width in reed 22⅕".

Width after washing 20".

Woven length (measured under tension on the loom) 42".

Length after washing (cowl circumference) 38".

Take-up and shrinkage 10–12% in width and length.

Warp Color Order

```
        ┌27x┐
108  │   4   │   Dark Olive
114  │1│ 4 │ 5 │ Silver
222
```

Warping and Weaving

Wind a warp of 222 ends following the Warp Color Order. Use your preferred method to warp the loom for plain weave. If you warp front to back, while you are beaming the warp raise shafts 1 and 3 on a 4-shaft loom, shaft 2 on a 2-shaft loom, or the heddle on a rigid-heddle loom. Separating the threads from each other will limit the amount of sticking that can occur.

You will be weaving with 2 shuttles to create the checks, carrying the inactive yarn up the selvedge as you weave with the active yarn. Start each shuttle at the opposite selvedge so that the inactive yarn loops aren't all on one side. The loops of yarn are not very long and will be hidden in the mohair fluff after finishing.

Spread the warp in plain weave using a smooth, nonfulling waste yarn (see Using Waste Yarn, page 15) for about 3". Using Dark Olive Kid Mohair, begin with 6 picks of plain weave beating firmly (almost covering the warp) to secure the raw edge. Then weave the cowl fabric alternating 4 picks of Silver Kid Mohair with 4 picks of Dark Olive, beating lightly (10 ppi) to obtain a balanced weave and square the checks. If you are using a 4-shaft loom, raise the shafts individually (using a direct tie-up) to limit the tendency of the mohair warp threads to stick to each other. For instance, raise shaft 1, then shaft 3, then throw the shuttle. Raise shaft 2, then shaft 4, then throw the shuttle. When the cloth starts to wrap around the cloth beam, wind packing paper with the cloth to keep the layers separated from the tie-on knots and prevent them from distorting the cloth. Continue weaving until the fabric measures 42"; end after a sequence of 4 Dark Olive/4 Silver with 6 picks of Dark Olive, beating firmly as at the beginning. Weave 3" of plain weave with waste yarn allowing 3–4" warp length beyond the waste-yarn section for tying temporary knots and then remove the fabric from the loom.

Washing

Tie loose knots in the warp fringe at both ends to secure the waste yarn so it remains in place during the washing process (this will keep the fringe warp threads from tangling and matting). Machine wash with a mild detergent on a gentle cycle in warm water with a warm rinse for about 20 minutes (note that this amount of agitation works with my front-loading washer; make adjustments for your machine; see Washing, pages 118–119). Lay flat to dry. Remove all waste yarn; steam with a fabric steamer or an iron as described in Steaming vs Pressing; see page 120.

Finishing

The fringes at both ends of the cowl are tied together to make the cowl shape, and beads are added as the knots are made. Mohair can be slippery, even with its hairy texture. Tying a secure knot is critical, especially with the added beads (see Fringing and Beading). The beads can be omitted, but they add a pleasing weight to the front of the piece as well as a bit of sparkle. When you are choosing beads to attach to the fringe, make sure the hole is large enough to slide a few ends of yarn through it.

When the cowl is worn turned down around the neck, the inside of this "seam" shows (the beads knotted in the fringe and the fringe ends are on the outside). Small beads are sewn along the inside seam line of this cowl.

FRINGING AND BEADING

1 Bring the fringes from each raw edge of the cowl together, matching the warp colors. Take 2 warp ends from each edge (4 total ends) and make the first half of a square knot, pulling firmly.

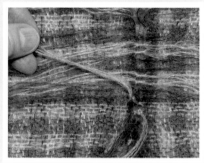

2 For a fringe with a bead, slip a bead onto the 4 ends you just tied with the first half of a square knot and tie them together with an overhand knot.

3 For a fringe without a bead, tie the 4 ends you tied with the first half of a square knot together in an overhand knot.

4 Alternate three 4-end groups without beads with one 4-end group with a bead 28 times. When all of the fringe is tied, clip the ends to 2" in length.

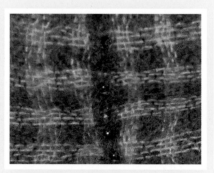

5 Sew small beads along the inside seam line, spacing them as desired.

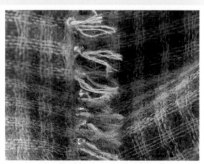

6 The beads and fringe lie along the outside seam as a decorative finish.

Blooming Scarf

DESIGN NOTE

I chose a flower for the embroidered design because the motif is the same on both sides of the cloth, making the scarf reversible—and it's easy to do. Plain weave provides a natural grid for stitching, and there are many other patterns you can stitch. Substitute any embroidery or counted-thread motifs that are designed on a grid. Make a simple stitch template by drawing or photocopying the pattern. Place the image on the woven cloth to decide where to place the actual stitched pattern(s) before you begin stitching.

Making a fabric template and weaving a sample are as important to do for a scarf as for any other garment. This is especially true if you're fulling or felting the piece, adding a slit, or adding surface embellishments. For this scarf, I planned a slit near one end so the opposite end of the scarf can be pulled through it to form a natural closure. Because horizontal stripes run the length of the scarf with a plaid border at each end, the slit needs to be positioned so that when the opposite end of the scarf is pulled through the slit, the ends of the scarf and the plaids fall near each other.

EQUIPMENT

2-shaft loom, 4-shaft loom, or rigid-heddle loom, 11" weaving width; 6-dent reed or rigid heddle; 2 shuttles; tapestry needle for embroidery and buttonhole stitch.

MATERIALS

Warp 2-ply wool (900 yd/lb, 1,816 m/kg, Harrisville Highland, Harrisville Designs), Sand #43, 95 yd; Toffee #52, 60 yd.

Weft 2-ply wool, Sand #43, 130 yd; Toffee #52, 22 yd.

Other (for embroidery) Kid mohair/nylon blend (70% kid mohair, 30% nylon, 4,450 yd/lb, 8,980 m/kg, Kid Mohair Lace Weight, Louet), Coral, about 16 yd

WARP MEASUREMENTS

Total warp ends 62 (see Warp Color Order).

Warp length 2½ yd (allows for take-up, shrinkage, and 27" loom waste).

SETTS

EPI 6.
PPI 8.

FABRIC MEASUREMENTS

Width in reed 10⅓".

Width after washing 7¾".

Woven length (measured under tension on the loom) 59" plus 3" sections at beginning and end.

Length after washing 48" plus 1" fringe at each end.

Take-up and shrinkage 24% in width and length.

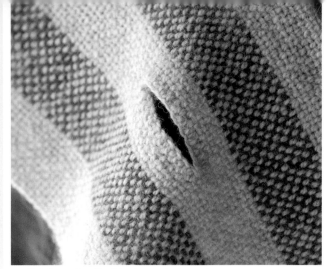

Reinforce the slit with a buttonhole stitch.

Weaving

Wind a warp of 62 ends following the Warp Color Order. Use your preferred method to warp the loom for plain weave.

Spread the warp in plain weave with a smooth nonfulling waste yarn (see Using Waste Yarn, page 15) for about 3". Weave with Sand or Toffee wool following the Weft Color Order. All numbers indicate inches of woven length except the first and last 3 picks. Beat these 3 picks firmly for a secure edge. Aim for 7–8 ppi and measure the 2" weft stripes carefully, changing colors when stripe height reaches 2" measured under tension. To begin and end weft threads, I recommend wet splicing (see page 93) even at color changes because it produces a smooth transition from one color to the next.

To form the slit: For 3", use 2 shuttles with Sand wool (see Weaving a Slit, page 91). With 1 shuttle, weave from one selvedge to the center of the scarf and back to that selvedge, with the other shuttle from the opposite selvedge to the center of the scarf and back. At the end of the 3", again follow the Weft Color Order using 1 shuttle with Sand or Toffee from selvedge to selvedge. End with 3" plain weave with waste yarn. Remove the fabric from the loom, leaving enough warp beyond the waste yarn at each end to tie temporary knots in the warp.

Washing

Tie loose knots in the warp to secure the waste yarn and machine wash with a mild detergent on a gentle cycle in warm water with a warm rinse for about 20 minutes (note that this amount of agitation works with

Warp Color Order

24	12	12		Toffee
38	13	12	13	Sand
62				

Weft Color Order

Sand / Toffee

3	
2"	
	2"
2"	
	2"
31"	
slit 3"	
8"	
	2"
2"	
	2"
2"	
3	

All numbers are inches, except first and last 3 (firm) picks.

my front-loading washer; make adjustments for your machine; see Washing, pages 118–119). Lay flat to dry.

Finishing

Remove the waste yarn. Brush the first and last 3 picks toward the scarf along the raw edges to secure them and then trim the fringe evenly to 1". Lightly brush the complete length of the scarf, including the fringe.

Embroidery

Using a tapestry needle and Coral Kid Mohair, embroider one flower (see Embroidered Flower) in each of the Toffee checks on each end of the scarf.

Because the slit will receive wear from pulling the other end of the scarf through it, reinforce it with stitching: Using Sand and a tapestry needle, work a buttonhole stitch (page 121) around the opening, spacing the stitches ⅛–¼" apart. Lightly steam the scarf.

EMBROIDERED FLOWER

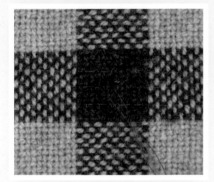

1 Bring the tapestry needle with yarn from back to front in the center of Toffee check.

2 Insert the needle into the upper left corner from front to back. Bring the needle up through center hole. Repeat Steps 1 and 2.

3 Insert the needle at the center top of the Toffee check from front to back and come back up through the center hole. Repeat.

4 Continue stitching petals to the centers of the remaining sides and the corners of the Toffee check in the same way.

5 When all the petals of the flower are completed, take the needle under all the strands of yarn, making a circle.

5 Go around in a circle one more time, pull the center tight, and fasten off the yarn.

Jean S. Jones

Handweaving is my love and anchor. It's where my heart and hands intersect. Weaving puts me in a space in which time itself seems to vanish into a rhythm of thoughtful process and slow living.

My journey began at my mother's sewing machine when I was very young. She taught me with a selflessness that is hard to find in modern life. I journeyed from that safe experimental place to learning to weave as a college student and later refined my skills by working in a weaving studio. I started my own weaving business when I was twenty-five years old.

From this personal journey, here's some encouragement to help you on your way:

Don't be afraid to cut your handwoven fabric. Start by weaving an extra yard or so for experimenting. Keep detailed notes about the yarns, setts, finishing, and shrinkage, so the fabric or something similar can be woven again if you choose. Then, because you have some extra to play with, cut some small pieces and sew some sample seams by hand or on a sewing machine. Are the stitches too tight? How does a curved seam work? How much seam allowance is needed? Do the cut edges ravel right away? Is the sett too close? A looser epi/ppi usually makes for a nicer drape in a garment.

Learn through repetition. Don't be too hard on yourself! If you make something you like, make it again. Or make something similar with a few minor changes. Keep detailed notes so that you can reproduce and improve on your results. Learning through repetition helps your hands know what to do and helps you refine your finished product.

Perfect your seam treatments. I find that for many of my handwoven outerwear pieces, a straight seam, sewn right sides together is the easiest and best choice. Seams can be sewn by hand, but I prefer using a standard sewing machine with a long straight stitch. I stop after each seam and press both sides, then gently press the seam open from the wrong side,

Keep detailed notes so that you can reproduce and improve on your results. Learning through repetition helps your hands know what to do and helps you refine your finished product.

then finally from the right side, always using a pressing cloth (and I've always practiced on a sample first). Leave the garment to cool on the ironing board with each pressing.

If the garment is not lined, the cut edges of the pieces need to be secured by overcasting. One option is to use a serger, if you have one. In the couture industry, it is very common to overcast by hand. No unnecessary bulk is added to your garment, and you have ultimate control over the process.

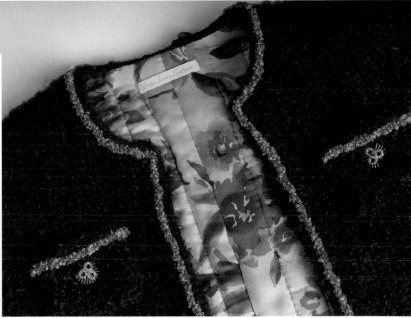

BOB FARLEY

KAREN J. DOWNS

JEAN S. JONES of Jean Jones Coutoure is a fashion designer trained in the classic method of French haute couture. All of her pieces are cut by hand, sewn one at a time, and finished by hand. Many of her outerwear pieces are made from her handwoven fabric. She lives with her family in Austin, Texas.

Heather Winslow

I look upon each of my garments as a three-dimensional sculpture that uses subtle simplicity to adorn the body and make the wearer feel "special" with the very act of putting it on.

I learned to sew as a preteen. It seemed a natural progression to use my handwoven fabric for garments. The leftover warp from my second project, a baby blanket, became my first handwoven blouse! It wasn't long enough, so I added knitted ribbing on the bottom and thus began my "finishing touches" journey. There are infinite ways that you can incorporate other fiber techniques such as knitting, crochet, spinning, dyeing, braiding, beading, and needlework to provide the finishing touch that makes each garment unique.

Recently, I've been especially intrigued with braiding. Slentre and kumihimo braids work well as trims, accents, buttons, frogs, ties, and loop closures. Takadai braids have the advantage of being wide and flat. The blouse shown on page 137 is trimmed with a takadai braid folded over the edges to encase them, making

Nature has always been an important part of my life and now provides me with most of my inlay design inspirations.

the garment reversible. The braid also has a ridge down the middle that appears as piping on the outer edge for an added accent.

I usually begin designing from the fiber. My favorite is silk, which I frequently paint to obtain the colors that inspire me. Turned twill showcases warp painting and adds complexity to the structure and shimmer to the fabric. Add beads and/or embroidery and you have a garment that is uniquely yours. What if you find some fabulous buttons? Think backward and create a garment on which to display them. You don't have to begin your design process with yarn.

I have been studying Theo Moorman inlay for thirty-two years and remain fascinated by its possibilities. The ability to weave an image of any shape or size in a specific location is always motivation to try yet another approach and make truly one-of-a-kind garments. Nature has always been an important part of my life and now provides me with most of my inlay design inspirations. I love to interpret what I see around me through color and texture.

When you design and weave, aim high. Extend yourself beyond what you've tried before. Each of us has a store of creative energy that can burst forth to surprise and delight us, given the right stimulus and opportunity. Don't be timid! Just as I have, you will make many mistakes. Make them with enthusiasm and verve and learn from them! Remember, the greatest inventions come from mistakes.

HEATHER WINSLOW's first love is teaching, and after forty-five years of doing so, she still finds great satisfaction in exchanging knowledge with students. She teaches weaving, knitting, spinning, and dyeing at the Fine Line Creative Arts Center in Illinois and at guilds and conferences around the country. She is the author of *More on Moorman—Theo Moorman Inlay Adapted to Clothing*.

Anita Luvera Mayer

My goal is to use historic symbols in a contemporary way as a means of honoring the women weavers who have gone before me and to connect my creativity with theirs.

The historic purpose of surface embellishment was to decorate cloth. The symbols used were often based on ancient beliefs and superstition. Designs and materials in the cloth of Shamanistic cultures reflected their belief in spirits and in animals as omens and messengers. Symbols representing the sun, the mother goddess, fertility, status, good luck, and more have been found on clothing and other textiles for centuries.

Historically, cloth not only adorned the body, but it also marked rites of passage and served as a means of identification as it still does in a few societies. It is this historic and ethnic approach to surface decoration that has been my source of inspiration. I use plain cloth that becomes my canvas for adding embroidery, beading, couching, and printing. My goal is to create simply shaped garments inspired by ethnic originals, and my clothing is my tie to a heritage and the women before me—a way of touching other cultures and times. It is how I communicate.

RYA EMBELLISHMENTS

On a trip to Finland, I discovered "rya," a Scandinavian knotting technique. Rya means "rough" and refers to the deep pile or nap produced by knotting groups of yarns to warp threads and securing each row of knots with plain-weave picks between them. I was also intrigued by the Scandinavian philosophy of using every scrap of cloth, recycling worn material by cutting or tearing it into strips for a new life in the form of a rya fabric. Although rya is not normally used in garments, I have added it to my clothing as a unique embellishment.

You can try this technique on your own for a simple scarf, adding rows of rya knots at both ends. Yarn, fabric, or ribbon can all be used for the knots, and you can choose their length depending on the effect you want. Any yarn in a threading suitable for plain weave for warp and weft should work for the body of the scarf.

ANITA LUVERA MAYER is a designer of contemporary clothing inspired by ethnic originals with all finishes and embellishments done by hand. She believes there should be something magical and unique about what is worn each day and shares that concept of clothing with others through workshops and lectures. Her work has been included in national and international exhibits, and she is the author of five books, including *Clothing from the Hands That Weave* (Interweave, 1984).

Yarns Used

This chart gives the yards per pound, meters per kilogram, and a range of setts (from wide as for lace weaves, medium as for plain weave, and close as for twills); no setts are given for yarns not suitable to use as warp.

8/4 cotton
(1,600 yd/lb, 3,230 m/kg)
10, 15, 18
Cotton Carpet Warp, Maysville
Saori Belts

Single-ply worsted wool
(183 yd/100 g skein, 837 yd/lb, 1,690 m/kg)
4, 6, 8
Donegal Tweed, Tahki-Stacy Charles
Checkered Sweater

100% handspun, hand-dyed wool
(110 yd/100 g, 505 yd/lb, 1,015 m/kg)
Naturwolle, Black Forest Yarn, Muench Yarns
Loopy Tabard

2-ply wool
(1,800 yd/lb, 3,630 m/kg)
12, 15, 20
Harrisville Shetland, Harrisville Designs
Striped Ruana, Wabi Sabi Jacket, Shades of Green Vest

100% wool
(131 yd/100 g skein, 600 yd/lb, 1,210 yd/lb)
4, 6, 8
Jackson, Tahki-Stacy Charles
Shades of Green Vest

100% wool novelty
(154 yd/8 oz skein, 308 yd/lb, 622 m/kg)
Mikado, Henry's Attic
Crème de la Crème Poncho

2-ply wool
(900 yd/lb, 1,816 m/kg)
6, 8, 10
Harrisville Highland, Harrisville Designs
Blooming Scarf, Crème de la Crème Poncho, Loopy Tabard

Wool roving
(130 yd/100 g skein, 595 yd/lb, 1,200 m/kg)
Montana, Tahki-Stacy Charles
Crème de la Crème Poncho

8/2 Tencel
(100% Lyocell, 3,360 yd/lb, 6,780 m/kg)
16, 20, 24
Valley Yarns, Webs
Southwest Wrap